The Portland
Book of Dates

The Port

land
Book of Dates

Adventures, Escapes, and Secret Spots

EDEN DAWN
ASHOD SIMONIAN

SASQUATCH BOOKS
SEATTLE

Printed in China

SASQUATCH BOOKS with colophon is a registered trademark of Penguin Random House LLC

25 24 23 22 21   9 8 7 6 5 4 3 2 1

Editor: Jen Worick
Production editor: Jill Saginario
Production designer: Tony Ong
Illustrations: Ashod Simonian

Library of Congress Cataloging-in-Publication Data
Names: Dawn, Eden, author. | Simonian, Ashod, author.
Title: The Portland book of dates : adventures, escapes, and secret spots /
Eden Dawn and Ashod Simonian.
Identifiers: LCCN 2020008572 (print) | LCCN 2020008573 (ebook) | ISBN
9781632173256 (paperback) | ISBN 9781632173263 (ebook)
Subjects: LCSH: Dating (Social customs)--Oregon--Portland. | Portland
(Or.)--Guidebooks. | Portland (Or.)--Description and travel.
Classification: LCC F884.P83 D38 2021 (print) | LCC F884.P83 (ebook) |
DDC 917.95/49--dc23
LC record available at https://lccn.loc.gov/2020008572
LC ebook record available at https://lccn.loc.gov/2020008573

Grateful acknowledgment is made for permission to use a representation of the following sculpture:
Page 76: Joseph Warren, *Diana's Stag*, 2007, Collection of Maryhill Museum of Art.

ISBN: 978-1-63217-325-6

Sasquatch Books
1904 Third Avenue, Suite 710
Seattle, WA 98101

SasquatchBooks.com

To Grandpa Jim and Grandma
Eva for showing us what seven
decades of love and
adventures can
look like

ZONE 1

Table

ZONE 2

nts

ZONE 3

ZONE 4

ZONE 5

An imperfect but, hopefully, helpful map

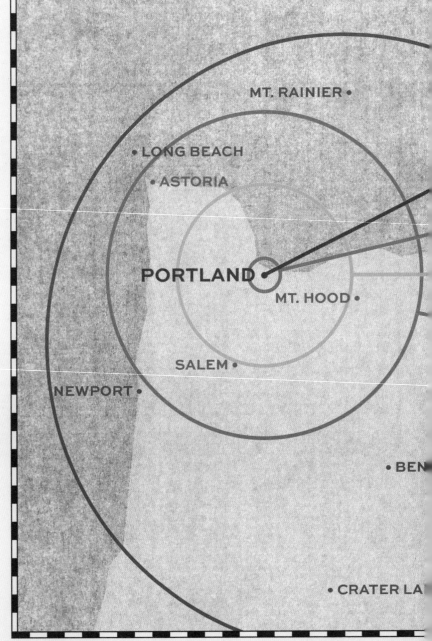

MT. RAINIER •

• LONG BEACH

• ASTORIA

PORTLAND •

MT. HOOD •

SALEM •

NEWPORT •

• BEN

• CRATER LA

ZONE 1
DOWNTOWN, NORTHWEST, NORTH, NORTHEAST, SOUTHEAST, SOUTHWEST

ZONE 2
THE BURBS, BORDERLINE, DEEP EAST, SMALL TOWNS OF THE SOUTH

ZONE 3
FARMS & FALLS, WINE COUNTRY, WATERWAYS, THE GORGE

ZONE 4
HOOD RIVER, MT. HOOD, WILLAMETTE VALLEY, COAST RANGE, NORTH COAST

ZONE 5
VOLCANOES, JOURNEY THROUGH TIME, HIGH DESERT, LAND OF LAKES, MID-COAST, LONG BEACH

NDLETON •

Introduction

We love being in love. With each other, especially, but with Oregon as well. Eden's been here her whole life, and Ashod moved to Portland in 2006 after passing through on countless rock-and-roll tours—always enamored by the cozy cafes, towering trees, and friendly people. We're both social types who circled each other's orbits for years before dating. We'd bump into each other at fashion shows, house parties, and backstage at friends' concerts, flirting across crowded rooms. When our stars finally aligned, we vowed to never become the kind of couple that spends every night in sweats zoned out in front of the TV.

That promise meant researching weird itineraries to impress the other and having a good time even when the weather upended our plans (which it did frequently, because Oregon). As our relationship grew, so did the amount of ground our dates covered. We visited places we had seen plastered on Instagram (hello, Painted Hills) but also stumbled upon some lesser-known gems like Clear Lake, where we floated in a rickety rowboat over a surreal forest frozen beneath the water. Our "Simonian Sunday Drives" (as Eden likes to call them—even if it's Saturday) became a regular occurrence.

Early in our relationship, Portland entered a growth spurt that has yet to show any signs of slowing. We lost our beloved neighborhood bar, Tiga, and every month since, it seems another favorite haunt is gone. While New Portland continues to rave about this hot new restaurant or that hip new bar—which, to be clear, are often wonderful—we are constantly making date-night arrangements to help support the establishments that made us fall in love with this city in the first place. We're including many of these within—not because we want to expose our secrets but because we want to share the magic we've experienced and help these places thrive for years to come.

In May of 2016, next to a glowing fluorescent waterfall deep in the recesses of the mine in the Seven Dwarves' House at Oregon's most off-the-wall amusement park, Enchanted Forest, Ashod took a knee and proposed. Our love has always been infused with an appreciation of all things kitsch, and there was no place more perfect to slide on a plastic ring and make it official. These only-in-Oregon oddities inform many of the dates in this book. Whether sipping from a fishnet-stocking-clad cocktail with Darcelle, the world's oldest living drag queen, or visiting an entire fantasy world methodically constructed from colorful rocks miles from anywhere, we always push to find the most fun and unexpected ways to spend time together.

We hope you enjoy the fruits of our labor as much as we did.

This introduction was meant to end there, but, as we were prepping files to send off for printing, a global pandemic changed the world. As we write this we are still in a fog of uncertainty. Will any of these beloved places be around when the book is released? Will we? Will anyone care about these silly date ideas? But then we see friends' pleas to support neighborhood restaurants by ordering takeout, people posting nostalgic pictures of their favorite wildflower hikes, and Zoom dance party invites. Oregon will likely look different at the end of all of this, but it's clear love and togetherness are here to stay and that is really what this book is about. We're lucky to live in this place and will continue to hold her up no matter what. We hope you will too.

WISHING YOU AND YOURS ALL
THE LOVE IN THE WORLD,

Eden & Ashod

ZONE 1

In Town

TO VANCOUVER ↑

← TO ASTORIA

North

Northeast

99E

Northwest

84
TO THE GORGE →

405

Downtown

26
← TO THE BEACH

Southwest

Southeast

TO SALEM
↓

TO MOUNT HOOD →

Downtown

Throw in Old Town and the Pearl District, and, technically, this is three distinct neighborhoods, but woven together, they make up the heart of our city. By day, downtown is full of office workers doing the grind, tourists living that sales-tax-free life, and folks clad in athleisure hanging at the lovely waterfront. At night, those groups disappear, while locals and the bridge-and-tunnel crowd roll in for music, theater, and cocktails. The plethora of options that await in our city center can be overwhelming, so it's best to break it down by what type of date you're in the mood for.

BOOK (AND NOOK) LOVERS

Few things are more attractive than an avid reader. Show off that big ol' brain in one of two ways. Option one includes a visit to the elegant Georgian-style **Central Library**, home to the Beverly Cleary Children's Library (yeah, Ramona Quimby is one of us) and the John Wilson Special Collections, where rare items like postcards from Allen Ginsberg and a special edition of *Geek Love* live. Each of you should reveal your all-time favorite page-turner to the other and then carry your conversation over to the **Multnomah Whiskey Library** to share more stories among the wood-paneled walls, soft lights, and roving carts of old-fashioneds.

Option two involves that tried-and-true

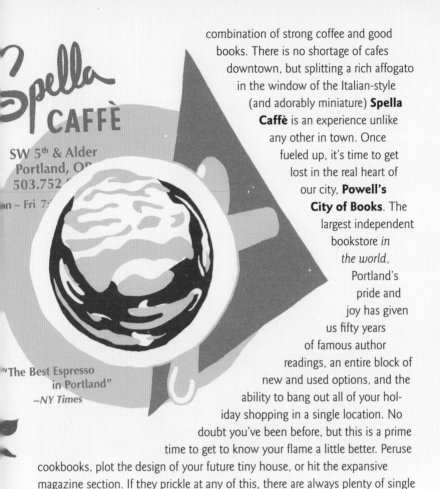

Spella
CAFFÈ

SW 5th & Alder
Portland, OR
503.752
n ~ Fri 7:

"The Best Espresso
in Portland"
~NY Times

combination of strong coffee and good books. There is no shortage of cafes downtown, but splitting a rich affogato in the window of the Italian-style (and adorably miniature) **Spella Caffè** is an experience unlike any other in town. Once fueled up, it's time to get lost in the real heart of our city, **Powell's City of Books**. The largest independent bookstore *in the world*, Portland's pride and joy has given us fifty years of famous author readings, an entire block of new and used options, and the ability to bang out all of your holiday shopping in a single location. No doubt you've been before, but this is a prime time to get to know your flame a little better. Peruse cookbooks, plot the design of your future tiny house, or hit the expansive magazine section. If they prickle at any of this, there are always plenty of single hotties with interesting eyewear wandering the aisles.

DESIGN AFICIONADOS

Portland is an indie fashion capital and home to all manner of amazing art. (Side note: Check out the annual **Design Week Portland** festival for a ton of events that cover everything from architecture to classic posters.) Put on comfy walking shoes and spend the day cruising around, seeing what the boss kids are up to. At **N'Kossi Couture Fashions & Alterations**, owner Jean Pierre Nugloze sells accessories

from his first home, Togo, in addition to making smart two-piece suits from colorful West African fabrics. Within spitting distance, find the oldfangled at the century-old **Portland Outdoor Store**, which still sells beautifully stitched cowboy boots and Stetson hats. Or go newfangled at "alternative medicine practitioner" **Serra** dispensary, whose modern, clean displays offer gummies and other legally laced delicacies to enhance your state of mind.

Make sure to pop into **Wildfang**, the feminist brand's flagship store, to pick up one of their iconic "Wild Feminist" tees and carve your names like lovestruck teenagers into the wooden graffiti wall.

Whether you're a bona fide sneakerhead or not, there is no denying sneakers run this town. In addition to having a nationally recognized Sneaker Week and the **Pensole Footwear Design Academy**—run by D'Wayne Edwards, one of the few people to have ever designed a Nike Air Jordan—Portland virtually requires that you stop into **Deadstock Coffee** for a dope espresso and to see where all the shoe aficionados hang out. Dive even deeper at **Compound Gallery**, where sneakers and streetwear are treated as art.

BOYS JUST WANNA HAVE FUN

FABULOUS NIGHT OWLS

While some of our city's nightlife activities are optional, this one is 100 percent not. In 1967, Walter Cole a.k.a. Darcelle proudly opened the doors to their drag queen cabaret in Old Town at a time when prejudice was rampant. For over fifty years, **Darcelle XV** with its hilarious, rhinestone-studded queens has been the spot to celebrate birthdays, bachelorette parties, or—simply—who you are. Darcelle is *Guinness Book* certified as the world's oldest drag queen (take that RuPaul!) and still struts her sparkly stuff alongside her right-hand queen, the incomparable Poison Waters, multiple nights a week. Come with open hearts and a wad of one-dollar bills, and leave with giant smiles on your faces.

Portland's history with jazz is long (The Dude Ranch! The Cotton Club! Jimmy Mak's!), marked by cool cats and sultry evenings. Walk through the leftover haze of ghost smoke that is the **Rialto Poolroom**, then pass the TVs playing ESPN and green-felted tables to the back staircase and descend into another world, the **Jack London Revue**. Down in this small hideaway bar, you'll find world-class musicians—some who are just passing through, like dance hall legend Sister Nancy, and others who call Portland home, like Mel Brown, a man so funky (he's played with Diana Ross, The Temptations, and Smokey Robinson) that Portland declared a Mel Brown Day.

Over on Fifth Avenue, the astute might notice a discreet door with a knock sign. Oblige it, and a bouncer will appear to escort you down a flight of stairs into **The Hoxton's Basement Bar**. The hotel's hidden speakeasy with embossed wallpaper and cozy leather banquettes oozes romance and a sort of mafia charm (in the best way). On the occasional Thursday night, young jazzbos squeeze their instruments into the corner of the living-room-sized space and deliver some of the vibiest jams in town. Finish the night on top of the world at **Tope**, The Hoxton's rooftop bar and its crowded-with-hot-people patio. F your L, you're one of them.

FANCY THAT

Indulge in a long, leisurely lunch at **Maurice's**, where the swoopy handwritten menu offers radishes with salted French butter, puff pastries, and rotating wine. Sit at the tiny counter and watch the stripe-shirted servers whiz about like they're in an episode of *The Great British Bake Off*. Up the block, indie film house **Living Room Theater** features La-Z-Boy-like love seats with a middle console that can be raised for grade A snuggling. Up for a fancy cocktail after? **Pepe Le Moko** is right across the street (and underground) with the award-winning concoctions that helped launch the worldwide craft cocktail craze.

The imposing walls around the **Lan Su Chinese Garden** make it easy to pass by without taking notice. In fact, it's a fanciful wonderland of orchids, speckled koi, and traditional architecture. Explore each thoughtful corner before entering the teahouse inside the two-story Tower of Cosmic Reflections for a cup of oolong and a moon cake. Plan ahead to get tickets to the garden's always-sold-out Chinese New Year festivities, where red lanterns glow and a dragon procession marvels the crowd.

HOT TIP: Tea and a beautiful walk sound just right but money is a little tight? Try grabbing a steaming cup of coconut milk chai from modern **Tea Bar** and taking a saunter through gurgling urban springs in tiny **Tanner Springs Park**.

More Fun

ONE FOR THE BOOKS—At the **Kinokuniya** book-store, find coloring books, manga, every type of stationery imaginable, piles of Pusheen plush toys, and heart-shaped cookies in the cafe.

BE MINE—A primo people-watching spot, politely elbow your way through crowded Ankeny Alley and the tourists standing in line for Voodoo Doughnuts, and then take a seat in the balcony at **Valentines** to watch whatever might be rolling through that evening, from poetry readings to shoegaze bands to throwback disco dance nights.

CAN I GET AN AMEN?—**The Old Church** is exactly what the name implies, but add a psychedelic light show and some of the best acoustics around, and you've got a remarkable all-ages concert venue that attracts some of the greatest names in the biz.

Northwest

The Alphabet District contains hot shop-hopping streets ideal for hours upon hours of window gazing and afternoon wandering. The neighborhood gives way to the elegant West Hills with our most prized park and the fanciest homes. It's bursting with beautiful old architecture, the kind that feels like you might be in Europe for just a moment, with something to covet on every single block.

SWIFT SWIFTS

Every September since the 1980s, throngs of couples, friends, and families have gathered at dusk to watch the natural spectacle that is the **Vaux's swifts at Chapman Elementary School**. While the sun sets over the West Hills, upwards of thirty thousand tiny birds swarm the sky, making their annual pit stop in Portland as they migrate toward Venezuela and Central America. What begins as an undulating mass overhead soon tightens into an impressive funnel, spiraling faster and faster until, one by one, the birds dive into the school's brick chimney to roost for the night. A. Single. Chimney. Additional drama abounds when neighborhood hawks appear from nowhere as the villains you love to hate. Onlookers gasp and boo collectively, cheering in unison when the last of the fragile clan is tucked safely into its chimney bed for the evening.

Go full heart-eyes emoji on this rare experience with a touch of advanced planning. Conveniently located a few blocks away is the cooperatively owned grocery store **Food Front**. Pop in for easy cheese plate fixins or have a couple sammies made at the deli. For prime bird-watching real estate, you'll want to show up ninety minutes before sunset to spread out your blanket. Find the best seats atop the hill above the soccer field—the level spots go quick. There's plenty of entertainment leading up to the main event with hordes of giddy

children zipping down the grassy knoll on cardboard sleds, and volunteers from the Audubon Society making the educational rounds.

After the last winged performer has taken its bow and autumn's chill has set in, warm yourself with a nightcap at Twenty-First Avenue's **M Bar**. This matchbox-sized wine bar fits approximately a baker's dozen, but it's somehow always possible to slip into a candlelit nook and disappear into a big, seductive red with your date.

WALK IT OFF

Chicago has deep dish, New York has bagels, and Portland's got brunch. Our bizarre obsession with lazy weekend dining has been the toast (pun very much intended) of countless food shows and even been skewered on *Portlandia*. The shiny new spots are doing a great job of expanding our city's palate, but sometimes it's best to remember the attitude of Old Portland that's on full display at **Stepping Stone Cafe**. From its origin as a soda fountain in the 1940s to its evolution into an all-American cafe in the late '70s, this eatery maintains the nostalgia with Formica countertops and red vinyl galore but adds a bit of punk-rock attitude with KISS dolls that hang from the ceiling. The breakfast-all-day menu begins with the statement "You eat here because we let you," ends with "Go Blazers," and offers all the basic low-key diner grub from sugar-coma-inducing French toast to hefty three-egg omelets oozing with feta, mushrooms, and artichokes. Nothing is shiny or new, and that's the best part.

Once you've consumed your weight in hash browns and coffee, you'll want to channel the motto of gym teachers everywhere and "walk it off." The level of effort is up to you.

Totes Easy

Next to the train tracks and underneath the Fremont Bridge isn't the place you'd expect to find a stunning oasis, but there lies the **Pomarius Nursery**. Thanks to owner Peter Lynn's taste level as a Belgian who spent years gardening in Southern France, this stunning indoor/outdoor nursery is dripping with so much European chic, you'll wish you lived on the property. Wander around the perfectly coiffed Dr. Seuss–like topiaries, admire the succulent-strewn container gardens, or pick out a low-commitment air plant if you're too busy to water. They also rent out the space for intimate weddings if/when the time comes (no pressure).

Girl, I Want to Make You Sweat

To quote the American poet Britney Spears, now it's time to "work b---h." Apply that ethos to the adventurous task of hiking the four and a half miles round trip up to the cherished **Skyline Tavern** for a drink in the woods. This thigh-burning hike itinerary, courtesy of the fine folks at the Forest Park Conservancy, ambles along the less traversed Waterline Trail, froggers across a couple main roads, and is sure to get you and yours panting in the middle of the day. Keep in mind much of this trek is straight uphill, but there's truly no better way to enjoy this city treasure (which is about six times larger than Central Park, thank you very much). You'll be rewarded grandly for your efforts. Nestled high in the hills, the nearly century-old saloon is plucked straight out of the Old West and plopped down smack in the middle of one of Portland's most affluent neighborhoods. Grab a craft beer or—let's be real—chug some water, play a round of horseshoes, and take a breather under the giant pines in the backyard. The hike back to the car is all downhill.

GOOD FLICK HUNTING

No need to reinvent the wheel, just bedazzle the hell out of it instead. When it comes to the timeless "dinner and a movie" date night, Northwest has options. Find happy hour happiness by watching the expert chefs at **Bamboo Sushi**, the world's first sustainable sushi restaurant, create a gorgeous Green Machine roll with tempura-fried long bean, avocado, and cilantro sweet chili aioli. It is the stuff of dreams. If sushi ain't your thing but international cuisine still is, option two is to dive into the Old Portland haunt **Le Happy**. This tiny treasure box is cute and cozy with savory and sweet buckwheat crepes. Live recklessly and order a Nutella, banana, and Grand Marnier flambé for dinner. If you have the time, pull a game of Connect 4 off the shelf and demonstrate to your date you can win/lose gracefully.

Once you're fully gorged, follow the neon lights to **Cinema 21** like a tractor beam calling you home. Built in the 1920s during the Golden Age of Hollywood, this locally owned theater still shows winners. Known for supporting indie and arthouse films for decades—Gus Van Sant shot *Drugstore Cowboy* up the street and premiered it at Cinema 21—the three-screen theater generally has something for everyone. Enjoy entertaining ads for handsome local divorce lawyers before the feature and then canoodle during the screening so you'll never have to give them a call.

HOT TIP: Tommy Wiseau—writer, director, and star of *The Room* a.k.a the Best Worst Movie Ever Made—frequently comes through town for viewings of the film, including audience Q&As. Bring your own plastic spoons and roses to throw. It's a joyous thing.

delicious and dreamy

Le 🏮 HAPPY
Crêperie & Bar

1011

BELLY LAUGHS

Some dates are best with others, and this one is the epitome of that old "the more the merrier" adage. Best of all, it works year-round, from pouring rain to summer sun. First step: Grab the gang and meet at **Marrakesh** Moroccan restaurant for dinner. For thirty years, this spot has provided limber Portlanders with tapestry-covered walls and patchwork pillows to precariously perch upon. The décor (embroidered everything) and serving flair (tableside rosewater handwashing and acrobatic tea pouring) are what make this place unforgettable. Make sure to go Wednesday through Sunday when chiffon-clad and rhinestone-encrusted belly dancers shake it like a Polaroid picture.

Now the fire is lit. Get your moussaka-filled selves up the street to **Voicebox Karaoke** (reservations almost always required) to keep your own private dance party going. In your personal karaoke suite, you can get loud and proud belting Foreigner's "I Want to Know What Love Is" while locking eyes with your date.

SPRINGFIELD IS IN THE AIR

Nerd alert! Did you know our little burg sparked America's longest-running sitcom? Former Portlander Matt Groening finally admitted in a 2012 interview (much to our collective delight) that the characters on *The Simpsons* are,

in fact, Oregonians. For decades, the world speculated where the fictional Springfield was located, but spend a lazy afternoon on NW Twenty-Third Avenue and you'll wonder how this remained a mystery for twenty-three years.

Take the number fifteen bus up (Mr.) Burns(ide) Street and hop off on NW (Ned) Flanders. Okally dokally, neighborino, now you're in the thick of it. Head north on Twenty-Third admiring the tree-lined street and little shops nestled inside aged Craftsman houses. If Lisa Simpson were real, you'd likely find her at the popular study spot **Tea Chai Té**. Choo-choo-choose a spicy cup of chai and take advantage of the secret balcony for a bird's-eye view of the bustle below. Just up the street, you'll find **Goorin Bros.**, a haberdashery perfect for a rousing game of "Would Sideshow Bob approve of this hat?"

As you continue north toward Kearney Street—yeah, just like the cue-ball-domed bully!—give a loud Nelson-approved "HA HA!" as you pass the tourists waiting in line for ice cream at **Salt & Straw** (though an insider hack for the deliciousness is you can skip the line if you're just directly buying pints and then grab a tasting spoon).

The **Nob Hill Bar & Grill** on Lovejoy Street (that's Reverend Lovejoy to you, heathen) is probably as close as you'll get to a Moe's Tavern on this posh boulevard with jaunty little statues out front that'll remind you of Homer's pet pig, Plopper. But as Comic Book Guy famously pointed out, "Loneliness and cheeseburgers are a dangerous mix," so don't dawdle and continue along until you come to another establishment the reverend would surely disapprove of: the **New Renaissance Bookshop** and boutique. This free-spirit haven goes full woo in a way that only some cities can. Here, the delightful and helpful staff can assist you with everything from getting a tiny pineapple house for a fairy garden to astrological consultations (unless you're a Capricorn who doesn't believe in that kind of thing) to a staggering wind chime selection.

Finally, follow the alphabetical streets down to Q, for Quimby, the inspiration for Springfield's sleazy mayor. There you'll find the **Bull Run Distillery** tasting room, where you can sip on some moonshine and plot your own political aspirations. Before you catch the bus back, look up into the evening sky and see if you can spot the giant glowing letters of Montgomery Park in the distance. That's your cue to put your fingers together and say, "Excellent."

Best. Date. Ever.

HOT TIP: Whether it's your first date or your five hundredth, showing up at the door bearing a gift is always a knockout move. With the one-two punch of next-door neighbors jeweler **Betsy & Iya** and **Solabee Flowers & Botanicals**, you'll have no problem finding something truly special.

North

The treasure trove of NoPo, as we affectionately call it, is vast. There are the gems you might already know—the mighty Paul Bunyan statue in Kenton, the indie-rock haven Mississippi Studios, or the glorious St. Johns suspension bridge—but our so-called fifth quadrant is overflowing with many more jewels to discover.

PINEAPPLE EXPRESS

Do you love drinks served inside ceramic puffer fish topped with pineapple and flowers? At hot-spot restaurant **Eem**, the vacation-forward cocktails set the stage for the Thai/Texas BBQ main-show mash-up. Keep the flaming looks (and drinks) going with a visit to **The Alibi**. The blinking lights of the giant Vegas-like sign act as a beacon on North Interstate Avenue to entice you in. Open since 1947, this right-of-passage tropical-themed dive delivers with over-the-top décor and flaming scorpion bowls with multiple straws for sharing. Pore over the gargantuan karaoke binder and find an island classic—say, "Part of Your World" from *The Little Mermaid*—to impress the entire room.

ONE MISSISSIPPI, TWO MISSISSIPPI

What **Sweedeedee** lacks in space, it more than makes up for in ambiance. The plant-strewn breakfast spot serves fresh pastries, molasses-tinged bread, and drool-worthy breakfast burritos fantastic enough to justify the sometimes stomach-grumbling delay. Plan accordingly, and some of your wait time can be spent flipping through albums at **Mississippi Records** next door. Their eponymous label features rare and amazing reissues from across the musical spectrum.

HOT TIP: For many, the solo date is a highly underappreciated occurrence. Bring a book, snag a spot in Sweedeedee's bright window or next to the record player, and burrow into a tasty meal for a luxuriant treat.

A half mile away on N. Mississippi Avenue, dozens of locally owned shops create the perfect environment for an afternoon of pinballing around the neighborhood. Don't miss the eclectic collection at **Flutter** with its tables of tarot decks interspersed among displays of perfume and art books, or **Control Vintage** where you can noodle on analog synths and modulators Brian Eno style. To peep the latest in local art, **Land Gallery** has a shoebox-sized showroom on their second floor that always features incredible (and often affordable) original works.

Beyond the quirky window display of **Sunlan Lighting**, owner Kay Newell has been hollering out her signature phrase, "How may I light up your world?" at *every single guest* who has entered since 1989. And while a light-bulb shop doesn't sound romantic, this one, especially with its mood-altering night-light collection, manages to pull it off.

Feel like a cocktail or mocktail to wrap up the day? **Psychic** is co-owned by Amanda Needham, famed costume stylist responsible for Aidy Bryant's killer looks in the Portland-filmed *Shrill* series, which translates to the bar's hand-painted wallpaper, infinity mirrors, and stylish patio firepit.

PARKS & REC

It's perfectly acceptable (and wise) to have a handful of dates that are all about the F-word: "free." These babies are the F-word times two, meaning "free and fun." Shout out to whoever invented parks.

SKIDMORE BLUFFS—This is *the* spot in town to watch nature provide an award-winning sunset. Bike in and bring provisions.

PENINSULA PARK—The first public rose garden in Rose City, this stunning European-style garden with its rows and rows of sweet-smelling roses in every shade of pink, orange, and red imaginable has been a go-to location for romance for over one hundred years.

CATHEDRAL PARK—Each July, thousands flock to the Cathedral Park Jazz Fest, a free-to-the-public blues and jazz celebration, but this riverside park beneath the towering arches of the St. Johns Bridge is good for a leisurely stroll or some sweet Frisbee action all year round.

KELLEY POINT PARK—The driftwood-scattered beaches at the confluence of the Columbia and Willamette Rivers make for a lovely dog-date afternoon. There is no shortage of fetching sticks, and though humans are discouraged from swimming, most pups do just fine frolicking in these waters.

More Fun

GET SAINTLY—Each May, the neighborhood hosts an eclectic bazaar (appropriately titled the **St. Johns Bizarre**) with an old-fashioned small-town parade followed by rad bands. And come fall, strap on your lederhosen for **Occidental Brewing Co.**'s annual Oktoberfest, where you will find the best wurst and plenty of beers to cheers.

BUST A BUCKET—Get hip to our intense never-ending love for the **Portland Trail Blazers**. Grab a drink at the wonderfully low-key **Sloan's Tavern** and, if the weather's right, walk over to a game at the Moda Center. Rip City, baby!

ARE YOU READY TO RUMBLE—If sweaty men wearing costumes and bear-hugging each other sounds fun, swing by **Blue Collar Wrestling** night at the Fraternal Order of Eagles. (Similar aesthetics, but different fun on hand, can be found at the neighborhood bear bar **Eagle Portland**.)

LOVE BUZZ—Steam up an evening (or an afternoon!) with goodies from **She Bop**, a woman-owned sex toy shop that offers an educational, judgment-free shopping zone and monthly sexuality-related classes and workshops.

ON THE RIGHT TRACK—Passionate people are the greatest people in the world. Learn a thing or two about pouring your heart into something at the **Columbia Gorge Model Railroad Club**'s open house events each weekend in November. The basketball court's worth of labored-over miniature lands put *Mister Rogers' Neighborhood* to shame. Sorry, Trolley!

Northeast

Northeast Portland is our biggest quadrant, enveloping a diverse array of small neighborhoods. From gawking at the old homes in Irvington to the eclectic bars and shops of the Alberta Arts district to the storied cultural history of the King neighborhood—there's a buffet of good times to feast upon.

GOOD THINGS COME IN SMALL PACKAGES

We've all heard the saying "Good things come in small packages." But the after-school-special adage just might be onto something in the case of Alberta's tiny haunts. Start off with a big pour in the intimate underground wine bar **Les Caves**, located in the ancient boiler room of a long-gone theater. It's not easy to find, but in-the-know crowds pack the joint nightly. If you're feeling nimble, snag the couch nook, only accessible by light acrobatics, and order the Wineman's Pick. You get what you get, but there's not a bad wine in this hole.

Keep the loosey-goosey good vino vibes going at another tight squeeze down the street. The rich Georgian dishes at **Kargi Gogo** are the stuff of love, including savory broth-filled dumplings and bread boats stuffed with butter, cheese, and eggs.

NOM NOM NAMASTE

Show off your flexibility with pre-brunch vinyasa at **Woodlawn Yoga**. Once you're limbered up, lumber down the street and fill 'er up at **P's & Q's Market** and deli. This quaint gourmet grocer sells a handful of dry goods and a few baskets of produce, beer, and wine, but the real joy of it is the counter-service restaurant inside. Help yourself to coffee and be sure to order a side of the saltiest, most delicious fries in the entire city, alongside your breakfast of choice. Weekends often feature live music with local legends like Michael Hurley, an outsider artist made famous in the 1960s Greenwich Village folk music scene, fiddling and singing right there next to the avocados.

DINNERS & DRINKS

Obvi, we're not the first peeps to think of dinner and drinks for a date. Netflix wasn't the first to think of movies and making out, either. It's about bringing your own pizazz to an existing infrastructure! And we heart pizazz, so instead of hemming and hawing, try one of these evening itineraries instead.

At **Akadi**, Chef Fatou Ouattara draws from her childhood growing up on the Ivory Coast to create one of the only West African menus in town. Do not skip out on the addicting *alloco*, sweet fried plantains served with a tangy house-made sauce unlike anything you've ever tasted. Just across Martin Luther King Jr. Boulevard, you'll find the beautiful 1906 foursquare home turned bar **Beech Street Parlor**. Order a house-infused whiskey cocktail at the bar and snuggle up on a Victorian sofa in one of the upstairs nooks. Eclectic DJs, often members of some of Portland's biggest bands, spin vinyl nightly, meaning you'll get no played-out playlists here.

A swanky hanky-panky-inspiring option begins at the candlelit marble-horseshoe bar inside **Angel Face**. The hand-painted pink wallpaper here launched a herd of copycats, so it earned its trendsetting status. Tell the knowledgeable bartenders what you're into, and they'll craft a custom cocktail to your liking, no menu necessary.

Navarre, the sister restaurant next door, has the feel of an unpretentious European restaurant but with an ordering process more similar to a sushi joint. Tick off your desired small plates from the inventive menu and nosh in whatever order stuff arrives. If you've saved room, or heck, even if you haven't, a coconut-lemon-saffron ice-cream cone from **Fifty Licks** across the street makes for an extra-sweet final course.

Or flip the bird to fancy with a lo-fi night on Forty-Second Avenue. **Pizza Jerk** dishes up vintage pizza parlor vibes with arcade games and thin tomato-y slices piled with cheese, peppers, and arugula. Stuff yourselves until your sides split and then wobble over to the charmingly divey **Spare Room** for a Monday-night game of bingo where the progressive Blackout prize could be worth upwards of seven hundred dollars. Theoretically, you could *earn* money on this date.

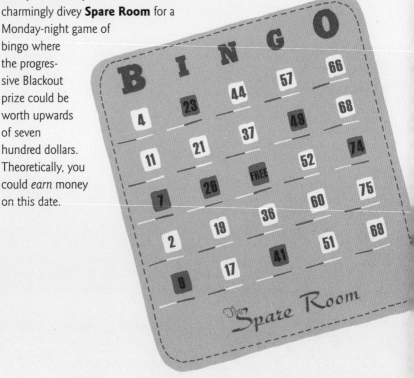

More Fun

CORNER SHUFFLE—The corner of Thirtieth Avenue and Killingsworth Street is a gastronomic hub. Start by taking a deck of cards to **Expatriate** for a friendly game of gin rummy while listening to records and sharing an appetizer before dinner at the stylish-as-hell **Dame**. Wrap it up with a drink at **Wilder** with the rest of the neighborhood.

DANCE YOUR ARSE OFF—Hot dang! A night of dancing is always a good idea. There's the amazing red leather banquettes and live soul bands at the old-school steakhouse **Clyde's Prime Rib**, or give **The Village Ballroom** a go for modern square dancing with gender-neutral calling.

GET CLIMBIN'—On Friday and Saturday nights, the **Portland Rock Gym** offers classes, harnesses, and rental shoes to outfit the two of you together. Then put your trust and teamwork to the test by climbing up their forty-foot indoor wall.

SEEING STARS—The gorgeous **Hollywood Theatre** opened its doors in 1926 with the silent film *More Pay, Less Work*. A century later, the nonprofit theater now screens new runs and boasts a number of highly entertaining special film series curated by local experts like Queer Horror, Fashion in Film, and Kung Fu Theater, each with their own preshow shenanigans.

Southeast

It is impossible to take in all that Southeast Portland has to offer in a day, or even a month. There are the pleasing gardens of Ladd's Addition, the rejuvenation of the Industrial District, and a dormant volcano with a view. Sprinkle in a healthy dose of Old Portland eccentricity, and this is an area you could spend your whole lives exploring.

THRILL OF THE (VINTAGE) HUNT

Portland is the queen of vintage. It has more shops hawking '50s frocks and mid-century modern chairs than some towns have stores altogether. Take a look around the pad, set a goal for the hunt, and commence a day of shopping along Hawthorne Boulevard. At **Lounge Lizard**, two nearly next-door locations of the same store, find groovy lights and the 1960s version of space-age furniture stacked floor to ceiling. Then pop into **Magpie**, where owner Todd Wooley curates over a hundred years' worth of women's and menswear but really excels at the add-ons from fedoras to funky, chunky bracelets. Fuel up on an espresso with a shot of chocolate on the roof of **Tōv**, a double-decker bus turned Egyptian coffee shop, where embroidered pillows and intricate textiles will make you forget what part of the world you're in.

Soldier on with stops at the massive sixty-dealer emporium **House of Vintage** and rooms of mid-century modern furniture porn at **Hawthorne Vintage** (Danish teak, yum yum!). Wrap it all up with dinner at the memorable **Sapphire Hotel**. Once an inn stocked with sailors running amok, now the candlelit spot is a place full of couples nuzzling over Whiskey Business cocktails (bourbon, Italian vermouth, and apple shrub) alongside fruity *fromage* plates.

LET ME SEE YOU QUIRK QUIRK QUIRK QUIRK QUIRK

"Keep Portland Weird" isn't just a bumper sticker—round these parts, it's a full-on mantra. Embrace the quirk with stops that could inspire an entire *Portlandia* reunion special. Comb through bins of octopus and lion door knockers, glass lampshades, and salvaged plumbing bits at the always-amusing **Hippo Hardware**. Belly up to the bar at **Fumerie Parfumerie** to order a . . . fragrance? The sexy red den offers free consultations to find your favorite new scent from indie lines including Portland's own Imaginary Authors and Slumberhouse. Just a few feet away on Division Street lies a witchy wonderland in **Secret Forest Books**. It's a dark cave with used alchemy books, a faux burning fireplace, and a proud Gandalf poster, and is definitely worth a visit.

A museum may sound like a basic date, but the **Zymoglyphic Museum** is a far cry from the traditional white-walled gallery. Open only on the second and fourth Sunday of every month, enter through the garage of curator Jim Stewart's Tabor neighborhood home. Inside is a weirdo make-believe cabinet of wonders, kooky fishlike creatures, and otherworldly dioramas constructed from natural materials but presented as preserved artifacts.

It's free, weird as heck, and you can spend as much or as little time as your brain can handle.

Nestle into a Christmas-light-strewn corner of the garden at the **Pied Cow Coffeehouse**, an exquisite Victorian that offers platters of Scooby Snacks for your pup, impressively cheap carafes of wine, and big, beautiful hookah pipes stuffed with apple tobacco. Or you can opt for the dessert route at the only-open-at-night **Rimsky-Korsakoffee House** where young folks eat slices of cake in the wallpapered parlor of a supposedly haunted house. Those observant will notice things are amiss, but we won't spoil your experience in advance—just go and keep your eyes peeled.

HOT & STEAMY

There are few things hotter than a restaurant that accepts brunch reservations. Impress your honey with no-wait gooey pistachio pastries and tomato-baked eggs with feta from the veggie-centric, Middle Eastern–inspired **Tusk**. The bright, airy space will set the stage for a day of decluttering your mind.

Hoist those happy bellies over to Finnish-inspired sauna **Löyly** to laze away the next couple hours. Trade your suddenly tight wardrobe for a robe and flip-flops and make the rounds between the dry cedar sauna and an intoxicatingly fragrant eucalyptus steam room. Recline side by side sipping tea and flipping through magazines in the tranquil lounge or go up a level for hydrating face masks and spruce foot soaks. Melt inside a salt-scrub shower before you go and carry the delightful warm feeling with you all day.

If the indulgence thing is working out for you, why stop there? Try on the ancient Roman lifestyle by gorging on more delicacies from the mastermind behind Tusk, Joshua McFadden.

Rather than dropping more dime at **Ava Gene's** (or do, not judging), pick up a copy of his cookbook, *Six Seasons*, and load up on fresh, organic ingredients just around the corner at **People's Food Co-op**. This lovely little grocer has been keeping the neighborhood's pantries stocked with nutritional yeast and soy curls for decades but does just as well with the newer generation of foodies coming through its doors. Be the "sous" to your partner's "executive chef" and keep the lip-smacking pleasures flowing.

DAMMIT, JANET, I LOVE CLINTON STREET

Tucked just off popular Division Street, the quaint Clinton neighborhood makes for a romantic bop around.

Step into a velvet painting at **Dots**, a beloved 1990s touchstone, for a no-frills drink in a dimly lit pub, or go a little fancier at **Bar Norman** with a rare natural wine in an industrial Euro-vibed space. For dinner, grab a booth at adorable **La Moule**, known for its wide selection of buttery mussels, but tbh, their salads and fries deserve equal praise. You might want to order an after-dinner espresso because just a jump to the left is the legendary **Clinton Street Theater**. Every Saturday night at midnight, this corner cinema screens *The Rocky Horror Picture Show* and, having done so continuously for more than forty years, retains the bragging rights to being the longest continuously running weekly showing in the world. Accept the lipstick V for "virgin" on your cheek and hold on to your seats because you are in for a real treat. Talk about a time warp.

A WONDERFUL DAY IN THE TABOR-HOOD

At the end of Hawthorne Boulevard, Mount Tabor, a surprising volcanic cinder cone jutting up in the midst of the city, houses a park known for its spectacular sunset views. Linger over a long French brunch of yeasty barley waffles at **Coquine** before taking an invigorating walk up the Tabor Steps (also known as the Labor Steps, so don't be surprised if you see very pregnant people huffing up to try and coax out babies). The almost two-hundred-acre **Mount Tabor Park** was Portland's largest until the creation of Forest Park and is always full of kids running full speed, badminton games, and couples lying out on picnic blankets. Pick your team.

HOT TIP: Every August, more than one hundred volunteers come together to produce the Portland Adult Soapbox Derby, where participants race their hand-built cars designed to look like hot dogs, video game consoles, and famous vehicles from your favorite television shows down the hillside to onlookers' cheers.

AFTERNOON DELIGHT

Everyone likes an afternoon delight. A little sweet treat is not only yums but also makes for an affordable low-commitment option for those awkward early dates. Even if it isn't a love connection, you get dessert, so it all works out in the end, right? The glass case full of precious selections at **Soro Soro** deserves some attention, but definitely opt for the snow affogato, a mound of spun sugar the size of your head with an espresso to pour over that deflates it into a flamazing sugary coffee treat with the flair of a Meryl Streep performance. At the Japanese deli counter **Giraffe**, try a plum-filled *onigiri* or—you're just going to have to trust us on this one—a little tea sandwich with hints of wasabi on the fluffiest, softest bread ever with a whole egg lovingly tucked inside. Bonus: **Cargo**, the two-story warehouse that houses Giraffe, is full of wonders from around the world, including rows of vintage kimonos, Balinese jewelry, salvaged engraved doors from India, and Día de los Muertos statues—it's the best browsing in the city, no contest.

And you can't go wrong with a visit to the Brit-owned **Toffee Club** where soccer rules. Grab a pint of Stella and watch some goals with an always-enthusiastic group of onlookers. Whoever's team loses pays the tab.

More Fun

THE FULL MONTAVILLA—If your date is cute and unpretentious, take them to the little Montavilla neighborhood. Go for piles of pita and pools of hummus at **Ya Hala**, followed by a trip to the historic **Academy Theater**, where movie tickets are so cheap it'll feel like you snuck in.

IT'S SHOWTIME—Share a boozy tropical slushie at the fern-filled **Hey Love** inside the Jupiter Next hotel, then mosey across the street to the *Twin Peaks*–inspired **Doug Fir Lounge** for a live show of a band you both love.

DOMESTI-CITY: POPULATION TWO—Bob Vila meets Martha Stewart. Pay a visit to **Mr. Plywood** for the supplies to build a simple garden box together (it's just four or five pieces of wood and some brackets, you can do it!) before a visit to **Portland Nursery** to pick out some stunners to stuff it with.

GET OUT—The challenge of working together against the clock in an escape room might be equivalent to six months of couples therapy. So . . . perfect date! Eschew the super-violent ones for the incredible tricky devices within the silly "Cat Lady" room at **Mad Genius Escape Rooms**.

Southwest

As you might've gathered by now, Portlanders love their parks. We devote large swaths of land to flowers and greenery, and Southwest has some darlings. A hillside with a zillion rosebuds opening each spring, an impressively authentic Japanese garden nestled in a forest, and city slopes zigzagged with nature trails are just a few of our favorite things.

GARDEN VARIETY

High above downtown sits **Washington Park**, 410 acres of secret gardens, wooded paths, and play areas carved into the steep hillside. See for yourselves why Portland is dubbed the City of Roses at the **International Rose Test Garden**. We earn that rep hard with all the rows of sweet-smelling summertime blooms (over ten thousand varieties!) that rise to a Mr. Darcy in *Pride and*

Prejudice level of charming. Just as the floral fireworks are bursting each June, drag queens take over the area for Peacock in the Park, a massive sequins-and-feathers variety show that benefits LGBTQ+ students.

Across the street from the garden, discover an entirely different zen world at the **Portland Japanese Garden**, where an hour's stroll will result in peace, harmony, and tranquility. Former ambassador Nobuo Matsunaga called it "the most beautiful and authentic Japanese garden in the world outside of Japan." Return through the seasons for full effect, and for a truly cosmic date, keep an eye out for their annual O-Tsukimi Moonviewing Festival. Walk hand in hand around the lantern-lit grounds, take in live koto harp playing and a traditional tea ceremony, then grab a seat and prepare to be moonstruck when the giant orb rises over the mountain and illuminates the city skyline.

High up on the ridge above the city, **Hoyt Arboretum**, our museum of trees, quietly offers city dwellers the free chance to admire more than two thousand species of sturdy wonders. The "living laboratory," as they call it (sexy!), is nearly two hundred acres with twelve miles of hiking trails perfect for aimless meandering with your crush. In the spring, the **Magnolia Trail** hits a serious level of sorcery when flurries of blushing pink petals from these tropical-looking trees swirl through the air, creating the perfect setting for a first kiss, the "let's get a dog together" convo, or saying sorry for hogging all of the nachos.

LIFE BEGINS AT 4T

The city calls it the **4Ts Trail**, for trail, tram, train, and trolley, but why let the alliteration fun stop there? See how many *T*s you can rack up by tacking on tacos, Thai food, toddies, tea, Timbers, tickles, and who knows what else. Begin by hopping on the red or blue line of the MAX train from Pioneer Courthouse Square and take it to the Oregon Zoo stop, two hundred feet belowground. Pop up in the undeniably coolest elevator in the city and follow the 4T signs onto the Marquam Trail. It's a long haul, but this path will take you to the highest point in the city, **Council Crest**. Once you catch your breath, there are a few more ups and downs before summiting another peak, at which point you'll find yourself surrounded by the mountaintop campus of Portland's big-name hospital, Oregon Health & Science University. The cafe here is not a bad place to replenish your energy. The hard part is behind you but, technically, you've still got two *T*s to go. Climb aboard the **Portland Aerial Tram** with the bigwig doctors and other lookie-loos like you and zip down the hill inside this strange, swaying spaceship of wonder. If you've never explored the South Waterfront, now's your chance. Otherwise, catch our slow but relaxing streetcar (or trolley, in this tale) to people-move you back to the square where you started. Terrific! You've completed a big weirdo circle. Toast to your travels (and tired thighs) with triumphant tequilas at a table for two up in **The Nines Hotel's Urban Farmer** bar.

CAN I KICK IT?

You know what's freaking fun? Chanting. Also, scream-singing with hundreds of your closest friends. Also, shouting "GOOOOOAAAAAAALLLLLLLLLL" at the top of your lungs. You can do all this *and* see world-class soccer players in action at Providence Park. Now you can opt for the **Timbers** with the raucous Timbers Army swaying in the stands serenading their hearts out, but don't sleep on the **Portland Thorns**. Our women's soccer team has its own army, known as the Rose City Riveters, plus a handful of badasses—including Lindsey Horan, Tobin Heath, and Emily Sonnett—who have redefined the sport on the global stage as part of the multi-championship Team USA at the FIFA World Cup. That means we literally have some of the best players in the entire world, and you can bask in their greatness for the price of a fancy craft cocktail or two. Warm up with a hot coffee after a rainy game at the adorable **Fehrenbacher Hof** coffee shop, or cool down with a frosty drink on the big patio at the **Goose Hollow Inn** next door. Both have been holding down this neck of the woods long before the soccer heads moved in and are pretty rad on non-game days, too.

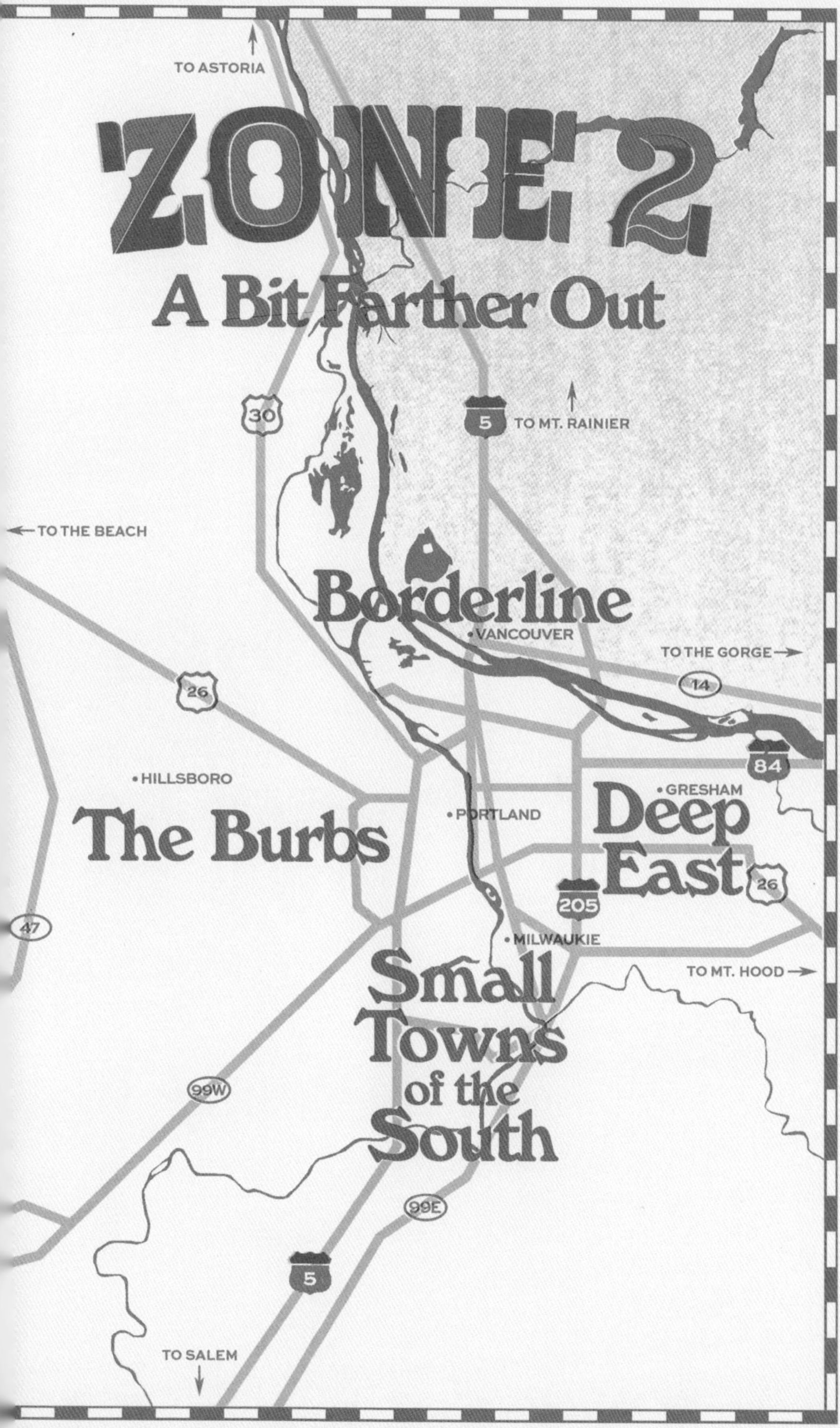

TO ASTORIA ↑

ZONE 2
A Bit Farther Out

30

5   TO MT. RAINIER ↑

← TO THE BEACH

Borderline

• Vancouver

26

TO THE GORGE →

14

84

• HILLSBORO

GRESHAM •

• PORTLAND

The Burbs

Deep East

26

47

205

• MILWAUKIE

TO MT. HOOD →

Small Towns of the South

99W

99E

5

TO SALEM ↓

The Burbs

Though some snobby types may not admit that fun exists west of the boundary of Portland proper, a little open-mindedness will prove it, in fact, does. A short drive or MAX ride will deliver city dwellers to some of the best food in the state (often without the long lines), and residents are already well aware that the sprawl means more space to spread out. Whether making a day of it, a life of it, or just stopping by on the way to the coast, it's time to get to know the burbs.

HOP TO IT

When the great American melting pot meets the great American pastime, you get a good ol' time. Trek on out to the **Hillsboro Hops** stadium to watch our beloved Barley the Hop mascot shimmy and shake while some guys throw a ball around behind them. (Pro tip: Follow Barley on Twitter for some real laughs.)

Whether it's before or after the game, take full advantage of the stadium's proximity to some of the best family-owned authentic regional cuisines available. At **Syun Izakaya**, try homemade gyoza, miso eggplant, or grilled mackerel inside a cozy pub atmosphere, that also happens to somehow be the basement of a library. Chow down on **Chennai Masala**'s addictive tikka masalas and chewy naan while Bollywood films play against the back wall. Or put your spice level to the ultimate test at **Taste of Sichuan**, where you may find yourself in a strip mall booth that screams of blandness, but dishes like Swimming Fire Fish are anything but.

ANCESTRY DOT CALM

Truth talk: Dating can be hella expensive. But the beauty of Oregon's, er, beauty is how many free, or at least budget-friendly, options exist. Par exemple: Have yourselves a sweet little history date that begins with an afternoon meander around **Elk Rock Garden**. It's the result of a lifetime of effort by Scottish immigrant Peter Kerr, who came to Portland in 1888, working and living here with his family until he died at the age of ninety-five. His daughters then gifted the home and grounds to the Episcopal Diocese of Oregon with the stipulation it always be free and open to the public. The cliffside estate features more than thirteen acres of paths that lend a bird's-eye view not only of the river below but also of a few enviable homes of 1 percenters. Stroll the mossy rock steps, admiring knotty, peeling bark trees and towering pines while catching peekaboo glimpses of Mount Hood across the valley.

A short drive away, you'll find **Barbur World Foods**, the perfect place to stock up on items for cooking a romantic dinner together. This locally owned store makes the usual shopping errand an entertaining afternoon. Aisle end-caps are dedicated to different countries, so it's easy to find Moroccan lemon preserves, Marmite yeast spread from Great Britain, or bottles of Brazilian Bode Amarela—tiny boba-sized balls of yellow pepper marinated in vinegar. Make your sweetheart something special, drawing inspo from your dad's Ancestry.com research or a country you hope to visit together one day.

FOREPLAY

Group date alert! Not only is it far more cost effective on this particular adventure, it's way more fun to have the crew watch your **Topgolf** swings. This national chain is the size of an airplane hangar: open-air bays provide the perfect tee to smash golf balls out into a field of light-up targets. Your group gets its own bay (charged by rental time instead of individual person), a server to keep beers and bites flowing, and a propane heater to keep it toasty even on a chilly day. It's kinda like bowling, but the ball goes a lot farther and you get to yell, "Who's your caddy?!"

More Fun

HONEYBUNS—
Oyatsupan Bakers' edamame
and sea salt rolls and drawings of
cartoon bears holding red bean paste
croissants and matcha buns make this
bakery one for the books.

GREEN EGGS—Equal parts plant
nursery and brunch cafe, **Cornell Farm
Nursery & Cafe**, a fifth-generation
family farm, prides itself on its
accessibility for all, fresh ingredients, and eight hundred varieties
of annuals and perennials.

**LET'S HAVE A
QUICKIE**—Named after the
original name of Puerto Rico,
Borikén serves big goblets
of mofongo, crispy *fritos*,
and pigeon-pea soup in its tiny,
colorful Caribbean-themed spot.
Adventurous couples would be well advised
to try a "quickie," Puerto Rico's preferred rum-
based concoction.

BIG FINNISH—On a sunny day, nothing beats **The
Nordia House**. Part of the Nordic Northwest nonprofit organization, the stunning grounds are home
to Scandinavian exhibitions and events as well
as a lovingly curated housewares shop and an
outpost of Portland's beloved
Bröder restaurant.

Borderline

Vancouver and Hayden Island may lie on opposite sides of the state line, but the river that separates them also binds them together. Hayden Island has a classic marina culture with jaunty sailboats and a laid-back attitude, while Vancouver sports a fresh multimillion-dollar waterfront renovation, leaving it with seven acres of pier-side restaurants and park areas.

NORTH OF THE BORDER

A cute mix of recently restored historic buildings makes downtown Vancouver perfect for a meandering stroll. It's always taco time at **Little Conejo**, where the team grinds masa daily for the freshest tortillas and the walls of windows offer a sunny setting to sip on one of their hundred different mezcals, either as part of a curated flight or in a smoky margarita. Help that digestive system afterward with a walk over to **Esther Short Park**, the oldest public square in Washington State. There are bronze sculptures, a little water feature to splash in on a hot day, and the impressive sixty-nine-foot-tall **Salmon Run Bell Tower**—a glockenspiel diorama that comes to life thrice a day (at noon, two, and four), telling a story of the Chinook peoples while dozens of bronze bells ring. Finish off with the handcrafted libations at **The Grocery Cocktail & Social**. Stop by on a Friday night for access to the secret woodsy-chic whiskey parlor in the back.

AN OFFICER &
A GENTLEMAN

In the fall, an afternoon walk down **Officers Row** is a gosh darn leaf-turning pleasure. Built in the mid-1800s to house army officers, these twenty-two gorgeous Victorians are now all on the National Register of Historic Places, and one of them, the **Eatery at the Grant House**, is a great spot for an afternoon treat. Named after Ulysses S. Grant, who lived at the fort (but not in this actual house), it's had multiple lives as an officers' club, bachelor's club, and a library. Today, its wraparound porch, manicured lawn, and beautiful wooden bar have just enough old-world charm to make this a destination worthy of the drive.

SUP, BABE

From the first sunny day in spring until Labor Day, all of the Pacific Northwest is in a collectively good mood, and much of this is owed to the abundance of water-based funtivities in the region. Rent a set of stand-up paddleboards from **Alder Creek Kayak & Canoe** and tour the weird and wonderful houseboats moored in the river. Should your abs need a break, the east end of the island offers a secluded sandbar with a stunning mountain view. When it's time to pull out (of the water, you scamp!), you'll have your pick of three nearby marina-side restaurants. We prefer the **Island Cafe** with its requisite pineapples, parrots, and piña coladas, but you can't go wrong with the fancy drinks and outdoor fire features at **3 Sheets** or the zero-fuss attitude at the (actually hidden) **Hidden Bay Cafe**.

More Fun

TICKLED PINK—**Alderbrook Park** is a private park that more than delivers on its ten-dollar entrance fee with a swimming pool, mini golf course, paddleboats, and—get this—a drinking fountain that flows with sugary sweet *pink lemonade*.

SPLASH MOUNTAIN—Technically a crater lake, though not *the* Crater Lake, the teeny **Battle Ground Lake** within a tiny volcano makes for a great, if not frenzied, summer swimming hole.

LOVEBIRDS—Every autumn, the Friends of Ridgefield Wildlife National Refuge put on the **Ridgefield BirdFest & Bluegrass Festival** in celebration of the sandhill crane returning to the region. Did you know birders love to party?

KNOCKIN' BOOTS—Portland's Portland-ness got you down? Escape for an evening to **The Ponderosa Lounge & Grill** on the edge of town. Tucked away in the Jubitz Truck Stop and catering mainly to long-haul drivers and country-loving suburbanites, this honky-tonk is keeping the '90s line-dance rage alive.

Deep East

This area's vibrant multicultural offerings make it one of the most fun neighborhoods to explore. There's the lively Portland Mercado serving up an array of Latin American cuisines, Korean diners that specialize in pancakes, and countless feast-for-your-eyes (as well as your mouth) international groceries. Plus baseball, begonias, and banjos!

MADE IN THE JADE

The Jade District was recognized as a neighborhood in 2013, and initiatives sprung up to support this Asian cultural district and its inhabitants from gentrification. Two weekends a year, the **Jade International Night Market** celebrates this confluence of customs with food vendors, maker booths, and entertainment. Choose from mouthwatering Burmese, Thai, and Indian dishes, and roll through the market on a shopping spree. Buy brightly colored crocheted earrings made by indigenous women in Colombia, geometric Nigerian textile accessories, and wares from ReSista Kat, a tiny cartoon kitty whose buttons and shirts let you know she is overrrrrr inequality and racist rhetoric (same, kitty, same). For dessert, grab a squeezed-while-you-watch sugarcane juice or boba tea and snag a patch of grass to revel in Cambodian pop singers, Bollywood dance troupes, and the always-smile-inducing Chinese lion dance.

Don't just wait for those two weekends, though: the Jade District is popping off all year round. Get yourself to Vietnamese soup stop **Ha VL** early in the day to find out why these spicy stews have such a ravenous following. Once they've sold out, you're out of luck. Then head to **Fubonn**, a massive grocery store and mall holding down the fort on SE Eighty-Second. Grocery shopping might not be the first thing that comes to mind when thinking of a great date, but done right, this place can be oodles of fun. Come with recipes in mind for a cozy dinner in, preferably ones with hard-to-find ingredients like enoki mushrooms or numbing Sichuan peppercorns, and let the scavenger hunt begin. Tack on some mochi for a special after-dinner treat and a couple tiger-themed Korean beauty masks to get you in the mood for a pounce. Rawr!

DIM SUM & THEN SOME

Two words: dim sum. Get thy hungry belly to **Ocean City Seafood Restaurant** any day of the week for cart after cart wheeled directly to your table loaded with things like steamed shrimp dumplings and golden fried sesame balls oozing bean paste. Sip piping-hot tea and enjoy the joyful din of Chinese and English chatter. If you've never tried a Chinese donut wrapped in a big ol' rice noodle before, you'll wonder how you've spent so much of your life without them. When you're just stuffed enough to regret that last steamed bun, it's time to get *your* buns outside.

The true love story behind **Leach Botanical Garden** can bring you to tears. We fully encourage reading the tale in its entirety on the garden's website, but the short version is that beloved local druggist John Leach and his wife, Lilla, an award-winning botanist who discovered fifteen species of plants, bought this plot of land in 1931, building out a fairy-tale stone house, a lovely manor, and gorgeous gardens on either side of Johnson Creek. When the lovebirds weren't building their utopian dream, they were off on botanical explorations in the mountains with their faithful donkeys, Pansy and Violet. See their lifetime of work six days a week for free. We're not crying, you're crying.

LENTS GET IT ON

The Lents neighborhood is a primo summer hang spot. Hit the **Portland Mercado** for a hub of Latin culture with Oaxacan, Peruvian, and Brazilian restaurants among the permanent indoor and food truck options, along with an incubator kitchen for newbies breaking into the biz. One special concoction? The spicy salted rim of the tepache with fermented pineapple mixed with Modelo at **Barrio**.

If your partner has BDE (we're talking "big dill energy"), go for a cheapy afternoon baseball game with the **Portland Pickles** and cheer for the college boys. Are hot chicks more your thing? Give the annual **Lents Chicken Beauty Contest** a go. It's just what you think it is, a beauty pageant . . . for chickens. Strutting their stuff are spotted Tolbunt Polish hens with puffy Phyllis Diller hair and white Silkie gals with such elegant plumage you'll feel them judging *you*. It's sweet and silly and, yeah, you'll definitely leave a vegetarian.

NECK IN THE WOODS

Each year, the **Pickathon** music festival takes over the **Pendarvis Farm**, with bands playing in barns, forests, and fields across acres upon acres of beautiful countryside. In addition to being the world's first big festival to go sustainable, banning all plastic cups and utensils, the curation of artists is always top notch, ranging from time-tested

superstars to up-and-comers before the rest of the world has caught on. Catch a local hip-hop band under the iconic sails on the main stage, head deep into the forest to sway atop a hay bale to some sweet folk music on the Woods Stage (intricately crafted each year from fallen branches), stop and say hi to a horse on your way to dance along with an Australian punk band in the barn, and then listen to a legendary soul singer under the stars. There are comedy shows, artist Q&As, and a children's tent, which often features big-name artists in an environment you'd never see them in otherwise. Follow the psychedelic lights up the hill at the end of the night and burrow into a single sleeping bag with your sweetie as you drift off to the soft strains of late-night crooners.

LIVIN' ON THE EDGE

We name-drop McMenamins properties frequently because the truth is they're good at taking old buildings and turning them into fun hubs. Their **Edgefield** farm is a prime example. Originally, the seventy-four-acre plot of land was a farm, then a nursing home, then abandoned dilapidated buildings set for demolition before the McMenamin boys bought the property in 1990. Now the historic buildings are all decked out with their own personality and tons of nuzzling ops.

The lodge has affordable rooms to stay the night, so it's an easy getaway or a place to crash after catching one of the concerts on the lawn from the likes of Lizzo or The National. There are par-3 golf courses, herb gardens to roam through, and glass-blowing demonstrations to witness. Or swim through the snaking channels of the fabulous soaking tub with palms high above and its own on-site cocktail bar. It's restricted to overnight guests *unless* you get a treatment at the spa (double pedicures, anyone?), and then you're allowed to soak and pamper all day. Finally, grab a drink and roam the grounds exploring each little nook and cranny—highlights might include a Led Zep documentary on the TV in **Jerry's Ice House** bar and a roaring fire in the **Little Red Shed**.

FLOAT ON

The childlike glee that comes with an afternoon of tubing the Sandy River should never be taken for granted. You'll need two cars, so gather a flamboyance of friends for all the necessary shuttling and drop off the first auto at **Dabney State Recreation Area** before you all continue on to **Oxbow Regional Park**. Then lash your air donuts together, slather on that SPF, and take off down the water for a four(ish)-hour adventure, laughing all the way.

Something about lounging in the sun and letting the river do all the work triggers the appetite, so once you dry off, keep the party going with some grub. There's the riverfront classic **Tad's Chicken 'n Dumplins** (which everyone around here lovingly calls Chic Dump) for the old-school Sunday-dinner options. Or try the newer **Sugarpine Drive-In** for artisanal chickpea and whipped feta salads, "waffle" grilled cheese sandwiches, or a giant mound of butterscotch-drizzled soft serve with sprinkles in a lively, bopping (read: sometimes crowded) atmosphere.

SUNDAY BEST

Cameo Café's Hansel-and-Gretel cottage vibes don't exactly reveal the vast cuisine offerings within. Friendly owner Sue Gee Lehn might have used the design brief "quaint English tearoom meets Korean décor" when creating this gem. You'll feel like you're over for family dinner as you see Lehn bustle about saying hi to all her regulars, and watch the cooks in front of you stack fluffy, buttery pancakes so big they come by the "acre." But the breakfast offerings are just half the menu; the rest is dedicated to traditional Korean options like kimchi and short ribs.

Three blocks away, **The Grotto** (officially titled the National Sanctuary of Our Sorrowful Mother, but no one calls it that) offers a peaceful post-meal walk that requires zero religious affiliation to participate. Take the elevator up to the top of the 110-foot basalt cliff and silently watch the planes come and go behind the floor-to-ceiling windows in the cliff-perched Marilyn Moyer Meditation Chapel. During the holidays, this place lights up, thanks to a kazillion Christmas lights illuminating the garden pathways along with a petting zoo, puppet shows, and the largest Christmas choral festival in the world featuring nearly nonstop choir concerts.

JOY

OAKS RINK

OAK
PORTLAND

SPARK

OAKS
RINK
ROLLER SKATING.
HEALTHFUL EXERCISE DELIGHTFUL PLEAS
OPEN. EVERY AFTERNOON AND EVENIN
LEARN TO SKATE
LESSONS F

Small Towns of the South

Things move a little slower down yonder. These little havens just down the road from the city center deliver charm by the boatload. Some are former independent towns swallowed up by a growing metropolis, some are quaint college neighborhoods, and some are just doing their own thang.

ROLL PLAY

Oaks Amusement Park has been an essential part of entertaining couples around here for more than a century. Sure, the old bathhouse and maze of mirrors with screaming skeletons are gone, but there are plenty of other vestiges from yesteryear. Let us direct you to the vintage roller rink, open since 1906 but with a distinctly 1970s feel. Pull on your knee socks and get ready to couples skate the night away. They have multiple theme nights a month—adults only with a live DJ, gay skate, and Saturday mornings for kids' tunes—so you can choose the pack you want to roll with.

HOT TIP: Cheer as hard as you can for one of our Rose City Rollers women's roller derby teams (including four-time world champs Wheels of Justice) while they kick ass and take names at The Hangar at Oaks Amusement Park.

RHODE SCHOLARS

The ten acres of foliage at **Crystal Springs Rhododendron Garden** make for a spectacular afternoon walking date. Twenty-five hundred varieties of rhodies, azaleas, and companion plants pop up around the picturesque bridges, winding paths, and lovely grassy patches. Stretch out a picnic blanket and unveil an *Alice in Wonderland* assortment of tea and treats while chestnut-backed chickadees and great blue herons act as party guests.

Across the street, at the handsomely manicured Tudor Gothic land of Reed College, Portland publisher Tin House hosts an annual **Summer Workshop** for burgeoning writers. Guests are allowed to wander into Reed's impressive lakeside amphitheater and listen to evening readings from notable workshop faculty like Lauren Groff and Tommy Pico while the sun sets and the bats come out to play.

SHIPS IN THE NIGHT

There is a critical precaution to enjoying this winter date—long underwear. You'll need it when you're standing in the freezing December night at the dock of Milwaukie Bay Park waiting for the **Christmas Ships** to roll by. Oh, but when they do! Thousands of flashing twinkle bulbs transform this fleet into a psychedelic holiday-themed light parade. It's a joyful sight to see the merry flotilla cutting through the dark night bringing festive lights up and down the Willamette River.

The second the captains turn their skiffs around, go warm those bodies. A five-minute walk, and you're in the door at delightfully hip **Decibel Sound & Drink**. Settle into one of the many cozy, low-lit nooks, order a hot toddy with a side of Nutella toast, and listen to the booming hi-fi sound system. You will thaw out quickly, especially if you cuddle up.

'TIL DEATH DO US PART

This is the most macabre date of the bunch, but ultimately, it's a love story. Each Memorial Day, for a scant *ninety minutes a year*, the **Wilhelm's Portland Memorial Funeral Home, Mausoleum & Crematory** opens the door to the **Rae Room**. If you make it through the door, you'll step into the final resting place of George Rae and his second wife, Elizabeth. He was

an exceedingly wealthy lumber baron at the turn of the century whose wood supposedly built half the homes in Portland. After his first wife was declared legally mentally unfit and died in the state hospital, he (scandalously) married his much younger housekeeper, Elizabeth. When he died in 1918, lawsuits and drama ensued, but eventually he was placed in the current tomb, and Elizabeth joined him in 1942. Now, together in their marble palace, complete with a stained-glass window that states "The End of a Perfect Day," George and Elizabeth accept fellow lovebirds into their final home once a year.

Outside the Rae Room, the rest of the Spanish Revival–style mausoleum—the first and oldest crematorium west of the Mississippi—is also open to the public on this single day. It features what seems like miles of impressive catacombs, ornate hallways, and impeccably decorated nooks. Sure, this can get a little heavy for a date with your steady, but it's an opportunity to be vulnerable and share some stories with each other about important people you've lost.

You can keep those old tales going a block away at the appropriately themed **Bible Club**. Nope, it's not a church, it's a gorgeous speakeasy tucked inside an old Craftsman home. The Depression-era décor is so spot on, it's easy to picture the Raes sitting on the antique couch. Dive into one of their simple platters and try a heritage cocktail as beautiful as the environs. To life!

ZONE 3
A Short Drive Away

← TO ASTORIA

↑ TO MT. RAINIER

← TO THE BEACH

Waterways

SCAPPOOSE •

The Gorge

• PORTLAND   • TROUTDALE

Wine Country

• McMINNVILLE

TO MT. HOOD →

Farms & Falls

• SILVERTON

TO EUGENE ↓

Farms & Falls

Rolling hills, pastoral fields, covered bridges, dramatic waterfalls, happy little trees. . . . Spending time in this region is like living inside a Bob Ross painting. Hop in your car, ditch your plans, and see where the road takes you. You may find yourself at a hilltop abbey, in a tropical sanctuary, or at a utopian commune turned antiquing hot spot.

PLANT ONE ON ME

Unless you've been sleeping under a rock with no Wi-Fi for the past several years, you're surely aware that plants are *very* on trend at the moment. But honestly, haven't they always been cool? From pioneer gardens to Grandma's pickles, hell, to the flower children of the '60s, the obsession with plants is evergreen. Take in any or all of these foliage-focused dates for a real sweet afternoon.

Mediterranean Delight

Spain is totes far, and it costs a pretty penny to get there. The how-the-hell-does-this-exist-here **Villa Catalana** winery, on the other hand, is just a short drive from Portland proper and offers enough old-world romance to warrant the trip. Once an empty hayfield, the grounds were transformed by married duo Cindy and Burl Mostul into a European paradise with picturesque ponds, a Mediterranean garden of olive and eucalyptus trees, and a rambling home based on a twelfth-century Romanesque church, San Clemente de Tahull. There are special chef dinners and Saturday wine tastings in their greenhouse of rare plants—plus, they let you bring your own picnics to fully experience the rustic setting. And just like when in rural Spain, you may need to defend your picnic from farm kittens, which is as cute as it sounds.

Flower Fields

Right around the time coeds are having margaritas mixed in their mouths on spring break, a different explosion is happening at **Wooden Shoe Tulip Farm** just outside Woodburn. Cars back up on the one-lane road and children run amok through the colorful fields of tulips, a flower once so coveted in the Netherlands it was *used as currency*. The only kind of currency the flowers possess now is giving you the best screen saver of anyone in your office, but, hey, that's not nothing!

As summer begins its long goodbye, we get relief in the form of the firework-shaped flowers at **Swan Island Dahlias**. Typically less crowded than its tulip counterpart, this is the largest dahlia grower in the country and produces new and rad varietals of the fancy poky orbs every year. Wander wondrous rows of coral clouds called "Jay Day," soft pink "Maui" blooms, and marshmallow puffs called "Bride to Be," then pick out your own bulbs to plunk into the soil together. And when those babies bloom long after you've forgotten about them, so, too, will all the memories of your blossoming relationship and special day together.

Botanical Buffet

Right outside the Mayberry-looking town of Silverton (there was even a musical about the town being home to the nation's first openly trans mayor back in 2008, Mayor Stu!) lies an eighty-acre flora smorgasbord, the **Oregon Garden**. This manicured beauty honors every kind of relationship with four miles of ADA paths, a children's garden with Frodo-approved hobbit holes, and even a pet-friendly patch where dogs rule the world (finally!). In fact, there are more than twenty specialty gardens—we're talking bosque, we're talking a steamy tropical greenhouse, we're talking lily pad ponds—to saunter through. And each December, it becomes even more magical when over *one million* Christmas lights transform the adjacent forest into a psychedelic winter wonderland.

FALLIN' FOR YOU

Silver Falls State Park, Oregon's largest state park at nine thousand acres, is an official must-do on the Oregonian bucket list. The three(ish)-hour/nine-mile **Trail of Ten Falls** snakes around—you guessed it—ten glorious waterfalls. But more than that, it actually takes you *behind* four of them. As in you can go steal a kiss under a freaking waterfall, which, tbh, is how most movies should end. You're rewarded early (and can easily bow out and turn back) at the first stop, **South Falls**, just a few steps from the parking lot. This 177-foot sensation is the star of the show, but once the fairy mist hits your face, you'll be transfixed and likely desire to continue on.

Ease back into real life with a relaxing bite at the sleepy little **Creekside Grill** right in the heart of Silverton. Request a seat on the back patio and enjoy a view of the creek and the covered bridge to complement your tempura-battered portobello slices, which go by the unexpected name Zombie Fries. Also unexpected is **The Grotto**, the restaurant's semisecret quasi-tiki lounge next door.

HOT TIP: While in Silverton, you may see a mural dedicated to its top celebrity, Bobbie the Wonder Dog, a border collie who famously sniffed his way back to Oregon after he'd been lost on a road trip to Indiana. In the midst of the Great Depression, the townsfolk decided to both honor the memory of their favorite canine and give the kids something free and fun to do by starting the **Kiwanis Pet Parade**. Now the longest-running pet parade in the nation, this ridiculous tradition can be witnessed on the third Saturday in May. See kiddos on toy tractors carting their prize chickens, little girls proudly cradling their beloved kitty cats, and fluffy ducks getting pushed in pink strollers. This may be the actual definition for the word "wholesome" and makes for an impressive first-date move for animal lovers.

ANTIQUE ROAD SHOW

When Preacher William Keil founded Aurora in 1856, it was a utopian commune focused on religion and music. It stayed that way for nearly thirty years. Now the small pastoral community is known for its superb antique shopping. Meticulously cluttered shops in historic farmhouses like **Aurora Antiques**, **Time After Time**, and **Home Again Antiques** are stuffed to the max with knick-knacks, tchotchkes, doodads, and thingamajigs, providing hours of entertaining browsing and the opportunity to trick out your first home together. Be sure to pay a visit to **Aurora Mills Architectural Salvage** for the most elegant version of a junk shop you've ever seen. Weird vintage signage hangs next to reclaimed stained glass panels. See carefully art-directed collections of ancient doorknobs and dress forms alongside an impeccable wall display of vintage wooden chairs.

Wine Country

With thousands of acres bursting with climbing vines and tart grapes, Oregon is heaven on earth for oenophiles. Wine country is ideal for the lushes among us, but with romantic cabins, a charming festival devoted to aliens, and hot-air balloon rides, it can also provide hours of entertainment for the teetotaler.

OLIVE YOU

Yes, wine country is about chilling out max, relaxing all cool, and shooting back some pinot outside of the school. While it's close enough to Portland to pop over for an afternoon, the best way to take advantage of wine country is to make it more than a day trip. There's loads of darling lodging options in the area, but for connoisseurs of tranquility, the cabin at **Beacon Hill Winery** is your spot. Situated at the highest point of the vineyard, the cozy cedar lookout tower is a marvel of carpentry with shelves and built-ins all along the tiny kitchenette up to the bedroom loft. Wake up each morning in the window-walled fortress and stare out at the hills of grapes like a sexy version of Rapunzel. The isolated feel of the little sleeper, despite being on the grounds of a working winery, is enhanced with Adirondacks around a firepit, a wrap-around porch with BBQ, and sightings of red foxes, porcupines (*porcupines!*), and skunks. Yo, Homes, smell ya later!

Though you can easily slip into the fantasy of being a prosperous vineyard owner prevailing over your domain, you might want to entertain the idea of leaving the cabin. Obviously, there are wineries in all directions, but the area's soil gives it up to more than just grapes. At **Red Ridge Farms**, you can experience all the fun of wine country without the hangover. The adorable and expansive grounds have gardens, groves, and gift shops—all connected by paver paths with swinging lights overhead. Explore the greenhouses, take a short hike through the olive orchard and around the property, and depending on the timing of your visit, watch workers mill olives into joy juice right in front of you at Oregon's only commercial olive-oil mill. In the solarium-like olive-oil tasting room, dip crusty bread into bowls of buttery, rich arbequina infused with rosemary and lemon. And if you really can't go without a little of the Big Red, they also have a vino tasting room with a tented and heated patio for sipping from their **Durant Vineyards** collection.

QUE SYRAH SYRAH

Once upon a time, Carlton, Oregon, was a logging town. These days, they refer to themselves as "Pinot Paradise," which sounds like something a drunk auntie calls herself at Thanksgiving. Find twenty-plus tasting rooms in the three-block downtown area, supposedly the most per capita in the country. Pop into any that catch your eye, like the delightful **Ken Wright Cellars** inside a renovated 1920s train depot, but the pièce de résistance of this tiny town is **Flâneur Wines**.

The local winery's tasting room opened in late 2019 inside an abandoned grain elevator older than Methuselah. Now it's an interior-design masterpiece eschewing the Olive Garden vibes of many a tasting joint for plush, hip décor and an impossibly tall exposed wooden elevator shaft. Crane your neck while polishing off a glass, and you may spot an eerie set of stairs near the ceiling that either lead to nowhere or to David Bowie's goblin kingdom (who can say?). An upstairs library area is particularly cushy with a choice people-watching view, and in the summer, the outdoor patio area is poppin' off.

In vino veritas translates to "there is truth in wine," which can further translate into spicy dinner convo. Spill that emotional tea to each other at **Earth & Sea** restaurant. Skip the "wine bible" and trust your server to pull a bottle from one of the super-small producers they champion. Then blather the night away over coconut bisques and house-made bucatini.

ONE-WINERS

It can be utterly overwhelming to know which of the never-ending vineyards and tasting rooms to hit up. Not up for all the Yelp-ing? Try giving tour director Niko Grimanis from **Works 4 Wine** a call. He'll cruise you around in a van to three sipping spots, doling out all the useful wine information (plus charm!) along the way so you can focus on a singular task—drinking. Should you want to go it alone, here's some insider info.

ANNE AMIE VINEYARDS—Our favorite scenic view to sit and quaff. Grab a cheese board and perch on the hilltop overlooking the Pacific Coast Range while taking in all their pinots (noir, gris, and blanc, thank you very much).

DOMAINE SERENE—The Disney Grand Resort of wineries. Not only is everything immaculate but the tasting room is a dining room, so no hovering at the bar for your next pour. You got parents coming to town? Take them on a double date here.

DOMINIO IV—Roses flank the old white farmhouse, and whites go down real easy on the porch. Reds are better sipped up in the creaky wooden loft over a game of H-O-R-S-E. Yeah, this might be the only winery in the region with a basketball hoop.

SPACE ODDITIES

Let's get into a little lore, shall we? On May 11, 1950, Evelyn Trent stepped out of her McMinnville farmhouse to feed her bunnies and tend the chickens. She saw a large metal disc-shaped object flying over the farm and ran to get her hubby, Paul, and a camera. The photos they snapped of the unidentified flying object went the '50s version of viral, meaning *Life* magazine published a story, the morning TV show circuit came calling, and the air force opened an investigation into the sighting. The town's reputation was cemented and McMinnville was henceforth dubbed "Saucerville."

Every May for the last two decades, little green men and foil-helmeted revelers have mobbed the streets at the

McMenamins Hotel Oregon UFO Festival. Cruise the main drag while avoiding eye contact with the handful of conspiracy theorists and tune in to the other 99 percent of delightful kooks who have descended on the town. There's a pet costume contest, weird VR rides, and—the real draw of the day—a parade with flying-saucer floats, marching bands, and Chewbacca tossing mini Milky Ways to the kids.

FOR RICHER OR POORER

Newberg really offers it up in the way of budgetary diversity. You wanna splurge for that big anniversary? Or maybe a birthday that ends with a zero? Let us tell you how to spend that cash faster than a gadget-loving dad the day a new Apple Watch drops. Step one begins at dawn with a visit to **Vista Balloon Adventures**. After your hot-air balloon inflates to life before

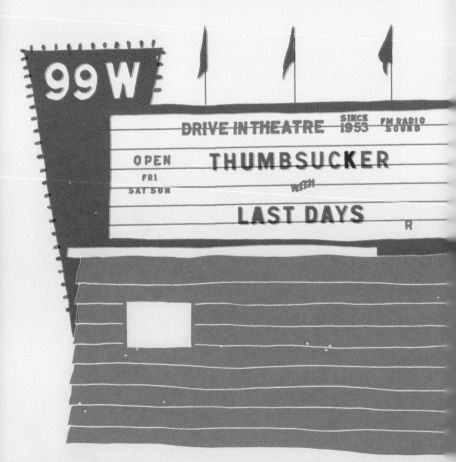

your very eyes, go up, up, and away, leaving all your worries behind. Sail through the sky marveling at the rows of vines abutting the dense pine forests.

Keep the wallet open for a plush overnighter at **The Allison Inn & Spa**. Everything about this extravagant spot is dreamy, whether you're taking a dip in the pool, chilling on the terrace, or going for it with double facials in the lavish treatment rooms. Absolutely make a reservation for dinner at the on-site **Jory Restaurant** for tender salmon and allllllll the wine. After that, feel totally justified to retreat to your room where a roaring fireplace and an Olympic-sized soaking tub await. Both super hot. Literally and figuratively.

Now perhaps the sultan's budget isn't doable. Hoo-boy, do we feel ya. And we got your broke back. One of the most charming dates in all of Newberg can be done for under a twenty spot. And if 1960s comedies are accurate, it's also *the* place for steamy car make outs. Nine dollars per person gets you admission to not one but two back-to-back films at the **99W Drive-In**. There are cute vintage dancing hot-dog cartoons before the films, OG *Donkey Kong* in the arcade, and a sweet little concession stand that sells cans of salty Pringles and pints of Häagen-Dazs (doubly delicious if combined). Bring a fluffy blanket and, for a good laugh, some Altoids.

Waterways

From mighty Sauvie Island and north along the Columbia River, this sprawling countryside makes for pretty views and exciting activities. This region offers up loads of date possibilities, from secret island campsites to super-freaky Halloween shenanigans.

WET DREAMS

There are plenty of places in the PNW to drop a kayak in the water, but for our money, **Scappoose Bay Paddling Center** offers an experience unlike any of the others. Rent your craft and make your way across the channel into island estuaries, which provide a snaking labyrinth of tiny waterways so narrow you'll be grateful your slim little kayak lets you limbo under fallen trees and through tall reeds while scouting for turtles and creeping on egrets.

A pleasant post-paddle watering hole is **Mark's on the Channel**. The floating Multnomah Channel dockside restaurant has an expansive patio so you can plop down and wave at boaters coming into their slips. Inside, a canoe hangs from the ceiling and the menu is full of the requisite fishy options as well as a delicious fried-cheese pita plate. This is a locals hang, so you might spy teens dressed up for a school dance and elderly couples swaying side by side while a live band plays "Me and Bobby McGee."

ISLANDS IN
THE STREAM

Sauvie Island is twenty-six thousand acres of bucolic farmland, sandy beaches on the river shore, and some of the best Sunday driving action around. Stop into **Kruger's Farm** to stock up on fresh snacks from their produce stand and roam the fields of u-cut flowers before visiting the gorgeous **Cistus Nursery**, where they've mastered hardy tropical plants so Oregonians can have a mighty palm tree in their yard if they like. It is an island requirement to visit the soft beaches and frolic along the river shore. You can opt for the famous clothing-optional stretch or go beyond it down to the very end of the line for a quieter hang with the breeze wafting as you chomp fresh blueberries and stretch out.

Want more of a walk than a sand nap? The lesser-known **Warrior Rock Lighthouse** is only accessible with a seven-mile round-trip walk that begins at the end of the beach where the sand turns into a dirt path that meanders along the river. You'll be rewarded with a view of our state's smallest lighthouse.

HOT TIP: Each October, the lines over the single bridge to the island goes berserk with folks all heading to the **Sauvie Island Pumpkin Patch** to get in on the hayrides, terrifying corn maze, and squash action. If you're just looking for a good carving pumpkin and not all the add-ons, skip the line by going the opposite way around the island to **Columbia Farms U-Pick**, a family farm with just as many impressive pumpkins but none of the kiddo stuff.

POP A TENT

Long-term love affairs need spontaneity just as much as when the infatuation was shiny and new. Only thirty minutes outside of Portland, the **Sand Island Campground** is perfect for an affordable surprise weekend. If you or your partner resemble the city gal in a Lifetime movie who has yet to discover the joys of country life, don't fret, this is camping with a dash of panache. After checking into the St. Helens Marina, a courtesy craft takes you and your first mate to a thirty-two-acre island full of nature trails and sandy beaches with equally sexy views of the mountains and ginormous ships sailing by. Wake up in your tent (the staff will actually transport your gear to the campsite with a people mover), lounge by the firepit, play a game of horseshoes, and heck, make out all over the dang place.

I PUT A SPELL ON YOU

When October rolls around, we have the just the thing for you and your ghoulfriend. Head north on Highway 30 from Portland, but take one quick detour just a bit past the Sauvie Island Bridge. Turn left on McNamee Road and motor up the hill until you come to the railroad trestle. There, you must pay the toll at the **Troll Bridge**. Truth. One side of the trestle has been turned into a monument to troll dolls with gnomes, hobgoblins, and sprites of all kinds hanging from a wooden shrine. Starry-eyed lovers are encouraged to bring their own spiky-haired monster to affix to the bridge for good luck. In future years, stop by when passing through and check on your weird little troll baby.

Some backstory: In 1998, the Disney Channel shot a film in St. Helens called *Halloweentown* about a teen girl who finds out she comes from a family of witches. Meanwhile, the neighborhood is filled with creatures of the night leading normal lives. Though this cinematic masterpiece barely made a blip on the national radar all those years ago, the city still goes *all in* during Pumpkin Times (officially calling the annual fest **Spirit of Halloweentown**). It's endearing. And when they shot a good chunk of the first *Twilight* movie here, it only encouraged locals more. All month long, the town square features various creepy photo backdrops like ghost dogs, Jack and Sally from *The Nightmare Before Christmas*, and even the original *Halloweentown* taxicab, complete with Benny the skeleton. If you're a Twi-hard, check out **Bella Swan's house** around the corner. And if you're the naughty role-playing kind of Twi-hard, rent the house on Airbnb for the night.

The Gorge

There is no shortage of beautiful scenery in the Pacific Northwest, but as far as unadulterated vistas that titillate go, this gorge really knows how to make your knees wobble. Generally lush and wet with waterfalls, the area is not immune to wildfire, as evidenced by the horrific Eagle Creek fire of 2017. The landscape has forever changed, but spring still brings the wildflowers; summer, the swimming holes; fall, its autumn colors; and winter—if you can brave it—frozen falls suspended in time.

GORGE YOURSELF

If climbing things like a mischievous little billy goat sounds fun, we've got GREAT NEWS. The Washington side of the Gorge has boulders and peaks aplenty for multiple dates' worth of thigh-burning intensity. Plan your trip accordingly (off-season or midweek), and you might skip some of the big crowds these trails can attract. **Beacon Rock**, an 848-foot basalt tower that's the "young" plug of a cinder cone, was purchased for the smoking deal of one dollar back in 1915 by local ecologist Henry J. Biddle, who built the amusement park–esque series of stairs and switchbacks that take thousands of adventurers to the top each year. While the elevation gain is no joke, this hike is relatively family friendly and unlike anything else in the region.

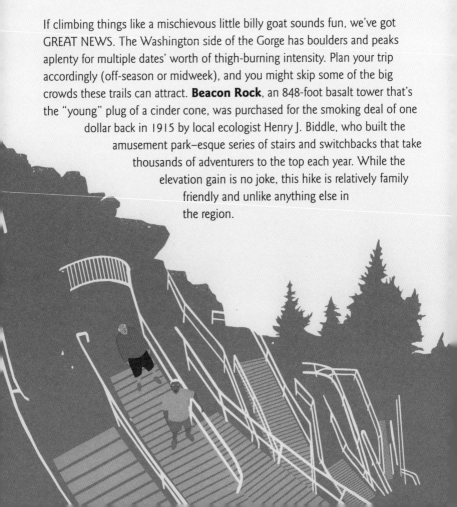

In late spring and early summer, flower-hounds flock to **Dog Mountain**, but the butt-busting six-mile trail is a great year-round option to get those hearts pumping. For your flora fix, check out the **Catherine Creek Arch Loop**, a two-mile loop that will still take your breath away but without the sore muscles in the morning. Or for some aloha vibes right here in the PNW, pack a plate lunch for a picnic in **Little Maui**, a lush glen reminiscent of Hawaii high atop Coyote Wall.

HIGH SOCIETY

Weekend getaways are the best, but sometimes it can seem like more time is spent getting there than enjoying the place. Chances are, your podcast will still be playing when you reach **The Society Hotel**, just about an hour out of the city. The Portland company (check out their other hotel in Old Town) took over the empty Bingen schoolhouse and turned it into a chic sleepaway camp. There are small rooms called "Math" or "Health" as well as über-cheap bunk rooms with immaculate shared baths in the hallway. But the grounds outside the schoolhouse are the real treat. Inside a ring of modern cabins (each

with its own hammock and picnic table)
is a luxurious lounge-your-ass-off-all-day
bathhouse area, which is free to all guests. You
can bubble in an outdoor hot tub, lay out by
a roaring firepit, sweat in a cedar sauna, or
gasp loudly in the icy plunge pool. Then do
the dang thing again and again, stopping only to head
to the on-site cafe for a frosty drink or pop into the gym
for a game of foosball.

If at some point your lazy feet get a li'l itchy, there
are options to fit the mood. Hungry? A mile up the road
in White Salmon, the **North Shore Cafe** has thick
smoothies and avocado bowls for healthy morning meals,
while **Feast Market & Deli** lets you take quickie lunches back to
your room or eat on-site at their pretty subway-tiled bar. Thirsty? Bingen's low-
frills **Chips Bar & Grill** has cold beer, a pool table, and a sign that says "Men
to the left because women are always right." Culture? A half hour east, visit the
random world that is the **Maryhill Museum of Art**.

The mansion turned impressive museum plunked down in the middle
of nowhere begins with local fancy businessman Sam Hill, who wanted to
build the house to entertain his school friend . . . the king of Belgium. You
know, that totally common thing. He also got most of the Oregon legislature
drunk to convince them to forge the Historic Columbia River Highway, he

built a full-scale **replica of Stonehenge** nearby, and for some reason there is a curated a collection of twenty-seven-inch-tall recreations of classic fashion looks from Balmain to Balenciaga. Oh, and there's a bunch of Auguste Rodin sculptures, too. No biggie. All that's missing are the peacocks that used to roam the grounds but had to be rehoused after aggressively demanding food from visitors.

DREAMBOAT

Longtime locals may scoff, but we say there is nothing wrong with dressing up and pretending to be fancy people from days of yore. Leave your Gore-Tex and Danners at home, counterintuitive as it may seem, and hop aboard the **Columbia Gorge Sternwheeler**, a 120-foot paddleboat. Look past the slightly stuffy décor (which could probs use a Joan Rivers–like face-lift); the real show here is the view of the Gorge from the dead center of it. Sit back with a cold beverage in a plastic cup while whimsical tales of river history warble from the loudspeaker system. It's cheesy, but sometimes cheese is delicious. Plus, it's one of the only ways to get a good view of the handmade platforms where members of the Yakama, Warm Springs, Umatilla, and Nez Perce tribes still dip-net fish for Chinook salmon. You can even pick up some of their fresh Native-caught fish in Cascade Locks, where the boat docks.

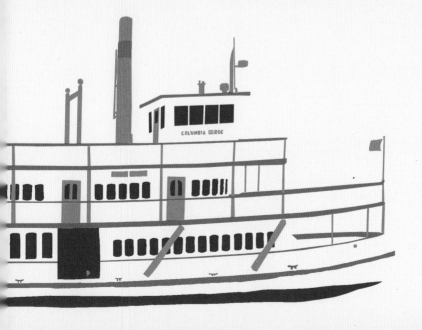

When you're back on solid ground, steal away to the spot once known as the "Waldorf of the West," a.k.a. the **Columbia River Gorge Hotel & Spa**. Opened in 1921 by timber giant Simon Benson, this hot-stuff hotel was once all the rage, attracting Hollywood movie stars like Rudolph Valentino, the 1920s equivalent of a 1990s Brad Pitt. A little stream with duckies runs through the old-world gardens in the front, but, unfortunately, the romantic vibe is soiled some by the "new" highway, which sadly made itself at home just a few yards away. Not to worry, the backside is totally bootylicious. The grand hotel is dramatically perched on the cliffs in a composition any landscape artist would drool over. Take a stroll over Zim Zim Falls, one of the Gorge's most overlooked overlooks, and then grab a spot on the patio for aperitifs—unless, of course, the piano player has clocked in, in which case forego the view for a litany of tunes guaranteed to keep you in those days of yore just a trifle longer.

JUST THE DIP

Since summers keep getting hotter and most homes here in the PNW don't have air-conditioning, a proper River Day is very much a part of local culture. Gather all your friends, your crush(es), and a cooler of sustenance and head out to stake your spot as early as possible. If you have the time, **OurBar** bistro in Washougal is great for egg-topped steamy homemade biscuits and cortados to fuel the soon-to-come cliff jumps at **Naked Falls**. Named for the nude sunbathers that once lounged like happy lizards on the water-smoothed rocks, this Eden-ish landscape of tranquil falls and deep pools is the far less crowded counterpart to its neighbor, **Dougan Falls**. Why? It's on private property, but the generous owner lets everyone in for the reasonable price of ten dollars per car, which is totally worth it for your own private slice of heaven (just be sure to purchase and print your permit ahead of time). Finish your perfect summer day with a stop on the way home at the floating **Puffin Cafe** for sailboat watching, tropical cocktails, and Jimmy Buffet vibes.

Speaking of naked, the other side of the Gorge boasts the special distinction of being the first clothing-optional beach in the entire country. Yay us! Rumor has it that when Lewis and Clark came gallivanting through the area, they essentially took one looooonnnggg look at the basalt obelisk thrusting its way to the heavens and named it "Cock Rock." At some point much, much later, the uppity nature of America took over and this beloved beach was given the more G-rated moniker **Rooster Rock State Park**. It's LGBTQ+ friendly and has soft sand, tons of private nooks, and shallow sections of the river perfect for leisurely wading under the beating sun.

More Fun

VANISHING ACT—Each spring, the South Prairie **Disappearing Lake** fills for unknown reasons to a canoe-able depth. Within weeks, it disappears down a hole just as quickly as it came, leaving a beautiful dry meadow with aspen trees and tiny irises in its place.

PINING FOR YOU—You might know Skamania Lodge for its cozy lobby, golf courses, and zip line, but the fancy **Skamania tree house** accommodations with firepits and king-size beds make for a wonderful splurge for that special occasion.

TAKE THE HIGH ROAD—The **Historic Columbia River Highway** is a winding drive, from the historic Vista House through dense forest and past several waterfalls, it drops you on the doorstep of the Multnomah Falls Lodge and never gets old (despite being really stinking old).

GOOD HEAVENS—Grab some take out and take it waaaay out. **Angel's Rest** is a popular hike, for good reason, but heading up late in the afternoon means you'll likely be able to find a secluded crag to claim as your own. Truly, the best seat in the house.

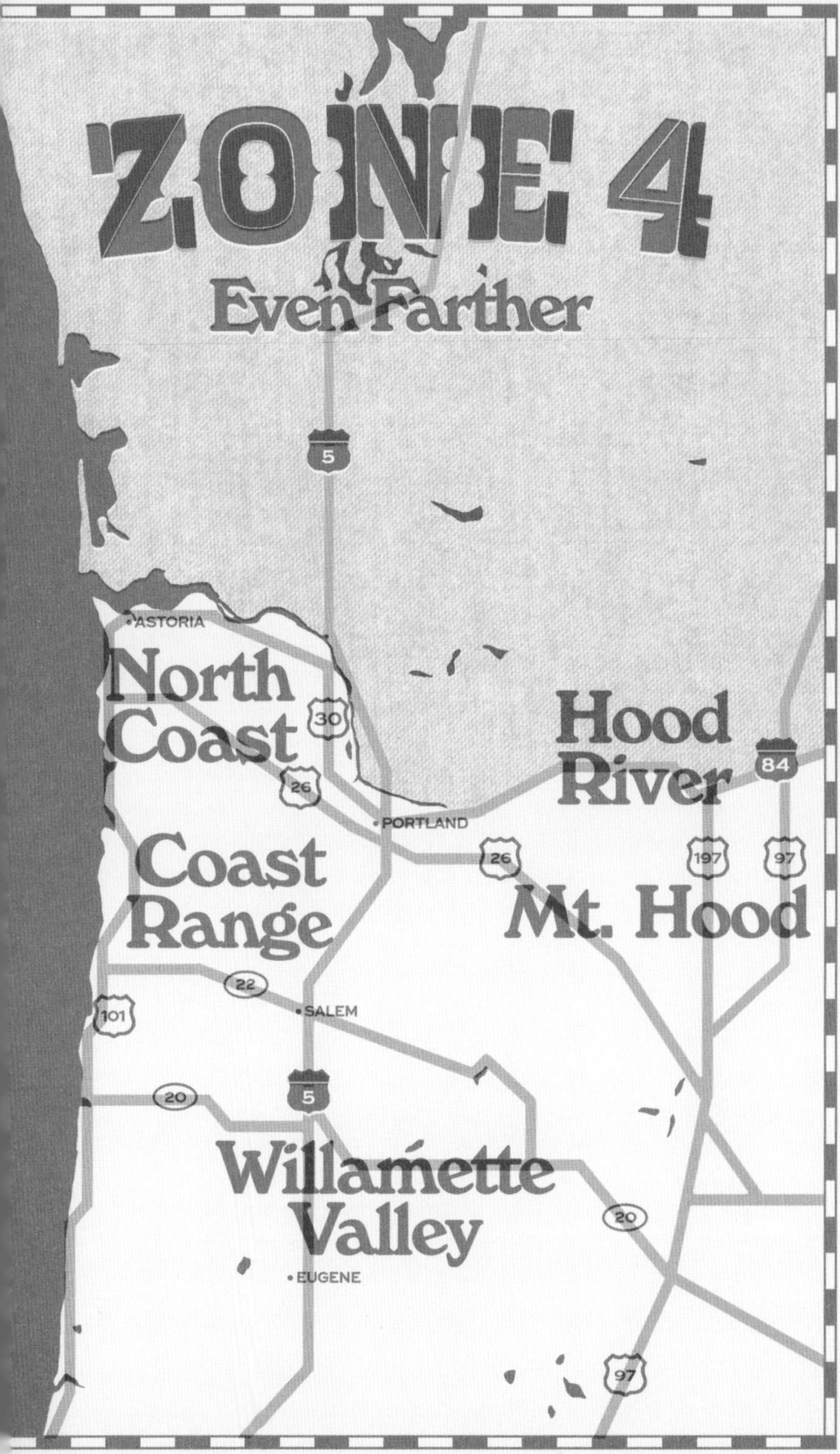

ZONE 4
Even Farther

5

ASTORIA

North Coast

30

26

PORTLAND

Hood River

84

Coast Range

26

197 **97**

Mt. Hood

22

101

SALEM

20

5

Willamette Valley

20

EUGENE

97

Hood River

Snuggled between the foot of Mount Hood and a wide stretch of the Columbia River, this fertile region features miles of such ridiculously gorgeous farms, flower-filled walks, and tiny country stores, you'll feel like you're in an antique train set. Spend a day scarfing cherries you pick from a tree or hike up a scenic plateau covered in nearly neon balsamroot.

FRUIT LOOP

You're likely going to wait an hour or more for brunch at most Portland hot spots, so we suggest a swap. Use that time to head out to Hood River and begin your day the Scando way, with aebleskiver doused in house-made lemon curd or lingonberry jam at **Broder Øst** on the ground floor of the historic **Hood River Hotel**. The sunny spot is the eastern outpost of a city fave that's frequently packed, so this is a two-birds-with-one-scone situation. After you've thoroughly carbed up, let the games begin. Before you hop back in the car, walk off your brekkie on **Oak Street**. The **Goodwill on Oak** is the boutique version of the thrift chain, **The Ruddy Duck** is a mini department store with full-on yard-party vibes, and if you like to travel with a Road Joe, **Doppio Coffee** can hook you up.

Just a few minutes into your drive toward our main bae of a mountain, pull into the colorful grounds of **The Gorge White House** for sensory overload. The historic Dutch Colonial is a hub of activity open to the ornate-molding-loving public while continuing to operate as a working farm. Spot fifty varieties of brilliantly colored dahlias in bloom, plus orchards full of fruit destined to become house-made pear wines. Grab a bucket and a pair of clippers from the fruit stand and head out into the fields to pick bouquets like you're in an IRL rom-com.

Before your hands cramp up, pop back to the car and head nine miles up the road to another picturesque estate, **Draper Girls Country Farm**. Along the way, give a gratitude wave to the **Juanita's tortilla chip factory** on Van Horn Drive. These angelic folks keep the Pacific Northwest stocked with the best tortilla chip in the universe, and it's a damn tragedy they don't have a tasting room to scarf down their indulgently greasy treats. Once you pull into

PICK

PICK

PAY YOUR GROCER FIRST

When you pay your Bills, Give your Grocer First Money, He supplies you with what you need, Food. Remember he Trusts You, Be Fair, Be Square, Be ⬤. Pay your Grocer First, He is not we⬤⬤ and nee⬤ money to buy more ⬤ood f⬤

We appr⬤⬤⬤⬤⬤⬤⬤ and if we make mistak⬤, gi⬤⬤ hance to correct them.

If we please you⬤⬤⬤⬤ neighbors; if not, tell us.

⬤ONISO⬤ ⬤rocer⬤ Co.

PARAG⬤⬤ ⬤RAD⬤
RE-ISSUED PAT. NO. 1262⬤ ⬤OR. 26, '07 ⬤ BY A⬤⬤ES BOOK CO LTD. EL⬤⬤A. N.Y.

POCKET LEDGER

86th ANNUAL EDITION

Compliments

MILES & ULMER CO.

the Draper parking lot, you'll be faced with a tough decision: Head into the fields of peach, apple, and cherry trees to show off your ladder skills and do some more picking, or just wander the grounds and take in the view? Regardless of what you choose, be sure to visit the pens of puppylike pygmy goats goofily prancing about and welcoming friendly head scratches through the fence. A few feet away, kiddos and grown-ups alike climb onto the sturdy tree swing and float about the bursting flower garden while gazing out at Wy'East (Mount Hood's original name from the area's Multnomah tribe). If you skip the full pick and hard-core pioneer homestead action, there is no shame in heading directly for the busy farm stand to sample whatever is in season, from dripping plums and tart raspberries to their famous cinnamon-sugar dried apples.

Take a break from ranch life at the southern tip of the Fruit Loop in the tiny town of Parkdale (population: 311). **Solera Brewery** has one of the most majestic open-air patios anywhere. Park yourselves at a picnic table in the backyard where the mountain hangs like a painted movie backdrop. Share a hummus platter or opt for their giant-ass burrito while you sip a dry AF cider, their popular Hedonist IPA, or stick with water to hold out for the final stop on the tour.

Fully rested and loaded up on vitamin D, it's time for the latter half of the loop. If you're a lavender lover, make a quick stop to run through the fields at **Lavender Valley** or snag some freshly made essential oils from their stand. The stuff is rumored to treat everything from acne to head lice, but really, just spritz some on your pillows before bed for a spa-like sleep and a touch of sophistication in the sack. Continue on past berry patches aplenty to stop at **The Old Trunk**. Originally opened in the early 1900s as a general store for area farmers, it's now an adorable soda fountain slash vintage shop. Strains of Arlo Guthrie play while browsers sip shakes blended with fresh local fruit and shuffle through piles of out-of-print books, horse paintings, campy records, and a rack dedicated solely to sequined things.

Just around the corner, you'll come to the so-cute-it'll-make-you-mad **Apple Valley Country Store and Bakery** for the final shopping stop of the day. Nibble tiny testers of their exceptional fruit jams and zesty pepper jellies (mmmm . . . peach-habanero) and, while you're at it, grab a slice of fresh picnic pie. Snap a rocking chair double selfie on the way out the door and continue on to your final stop of the day, **Marchesi Winery**. You've earned it.

Founder Franco Marchesi compares the snowy peaks of Hood to his childhood in Piedmont, Italy, situated at the foot of the Alps, where the rich soil allows them to grow barbera and pinot grigio grapes alike. Italian décor, including a mural of Piedmont, dot the tasting room and an ample patio where blankets, heaters, and the occasional furry kitty keep it cozy when the temps start to drop. While staring hypnotically over the rows and rows of vineyards, pretend they're yours and this is your life now.

MOSIER ON DOWN

Just east of Hood River, pocket-size Mosier (population: 500) was once an 1800s rest stop for explorers crossing Oregon. Come spring, the area bursts to life with wildflowers dotting its volcanic ridges. The trailhead for the three-and-a-half-mile **Mosier Plateau** hike begins right along the **Historic Columbia River Highway** that runs through town. Walk hand in hand along a dirt path with waist-high bright-yellow balsamroot and sweet purple lupine. Soon you'll come across a teeny-tiny pioneer cemetery with just a handful of mossy headstones from some of the town's namesakes. Pay your respects and move on a few short minutes to watch ambitious visitors jump from rocks into the cold swimming hole of **Mosier Creek** as it cascades into a waterfall.

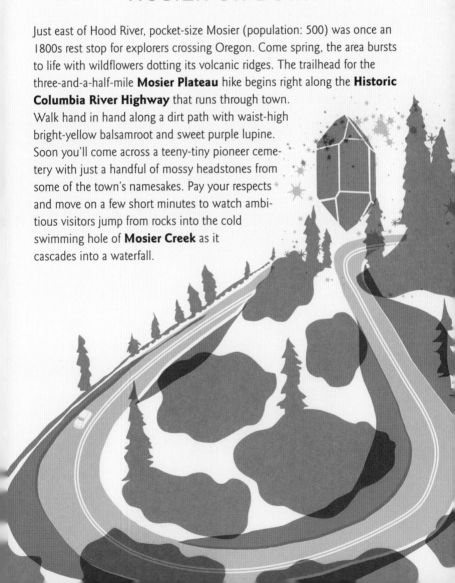

For the relaxation inclined, it's perfectly acceptable to just call it here and spend some time splashing around. But if views are the goal, the trail will provide. Soldier on through the fields of flowers up a set of switchbacks without an ounce of shade in sight. At the top of the seven-hundred-foot elevation gain, you'll hit the plateau to gaze down at the river rushing through the magnificent canyon.

Climb back down and give the wobbly legs a break with a lovely drive up the historic highway. The oldest scenic highway in America, it was formed over a century ago and dubbed the "King of the Road" for its stunning loopy, swoopy cliffside road—an architectural marvel at the time. Ogle the six miles of pines, colorful knolls, and family farms from Mosier up to Rowena Crest. Here, experience a strong hit of déjà vu from all the national car commercials filmed along this particularly beautiful twist of road as you get out and wander the vast opening of the **Tom McCall Nature Preserve**, or try to spot a windsurfer down on the river. Head back to town to grub up at the locally owned **Mosier Company** pub with an outdoor patio as big as the restaurant, wine and cider made from area fruit, and plentiful piles of Juanita's tortilla chips with every meal.

Mount Hood

This majestic mountain acts as our collective crystal ball. On the clear days we are lucky enough to see her stretching up to the sun from our city perch, we are reminded of all she offers: Disco sledding! Snowshoeing! Alpine swimming! And when the dark clouds roll in ominously, we are reminded that she is the epitome of nature, beautiful and dangerous if not taken seriously.

HUNKER DOWN

Henry Steiner and his thirteen kids left their mark on Mount Hood by way of building a hundred log cabins over three decades beginning during the Depression. Each of the cabins are different with the family crafting bendable trees into clever archways and river stones into grand hearths (see a bunch at once at the annual **Steiner Cabins** tour if you super-heart log cabins). Amazingly, a handful of these lovelies are available to rent direct from the individual owners on any of the big-name sites. Before heading up the mountain, pick up the card game Illimat, created in part by local stalwarts The Decemberists and illustrator Carson Ellis, and some Portland-made drinking chocolate from Woodblock Chocolate and prepare to hunker down in front of the toasty fire.

If the time is right, nothing beats the Chevy Chase/Clark Griswold level of pride in cutting down your own Christmas tree. Visit the ranger station in Zigzag or one of the local grocery stores to purchase a tree-cutting permit for the shockingly bargain price of five dollars. You'll be provided with a map along with instructions on which trees you're allowed to fell. Then go forth layered in clothing, hand warmers stuffed in your gloves, and saw in hand to find "The One." The selection might be a bit more Charlie Brown than your typical farm-raised tree, but true love isn't about perfection.

Defrost the toes and shake off the snow at the roadhouse **Skyway Bar and Grill**. Its motley décor, wall of hodgepodge stained glass, and colorful twinkle lights make it one of the more welcoming après-ski spots on the mountain. Their big BBQ menu, deep-fried pickle chips, and indulgent hot drinks make for the perfect end to a wintry day.

SNOWBIRDS

Mount Hood is a winter sports paradise, but hurtling down mountains at high speeds isn't for everyone. The less athletic among us can still get in on the action by renting a pair of snowshoes and moving at our own speed. **Trillium Lake** offers an excellent four(ish)-mile trail appropriate for total newbies, with stunning views and friendly gray jays to keep you company. Whether or not you get caught in flurries, you'll feel like you're in a magical snow globe. If you're looking to up the alchemy quotient even further, several outfitters provide moonlight snowshoe tours, but dates, which revolve around the full moon, are limited, so plan accordingly. Wherever your adventure takes you, make sure to squeeze in a visit to **Koya Kitchen** to warm your bones with a steaming bowl of hot ramen. Order from the truck out back and cozy up next to the woodstove with a green tea in the attached boho dining room.

TOP OF THE MOUNTAIN TO YOU

If you've never been to the jewel of Mount Hood, **Timberline Lodge**, the first time you pull up, it might look familiar. That's because the exterior was made famous as the Overlook Hotel in Stephen King's film *The Shining*. Built by the Works Progress Administration starting in 1935, the mile-high ski resort features all kinds of special touches like light fixtures made from cattle yokes, animals carved into stair posts, and stained-glass blue oxen. Do not be a dull boy like Jack, and go have a flaming drink at the **Ram's Head Bar & Restaurant**. The view inside, anchored by a glorious stone chimney, is as lovely as the view outside, so there isn't a bad seat in the house. The elevation is such that you might even be able to pull off a snowball fight in the peak of summer, which, on a hot Portland day, makes for a pretty cool surprise date. But go easy—by July, you'll be packing hard ice into balls, which is way less pleasant than a powdery winter puff.

PURE BATHING CULTURE

Get off the grid with a weekend at the secluded **Breitenbush Hot Springs Retreat and Conference Center** miles away from cell service, Wi-Fi, or civilization. They're so far off the beaten path, the zen retreat harnesses its own electricity through a geothermal well on the grounds. Get sweaty in the wooden sauna situated over a geyser with hot steam rising through the slats, or float in a silent rock pool beneath a sea of stars.

As with many other hot springs in Oregon, this was once a place for local indigenous tribes to commune and use the waters for healing, but the current name came in the late 1800s when a survey party found a one-armed Dutch hunter Lewis Breitenbucher living totally alone on the land. After several different incarnations, it morphed into its current hippie cooperative in the late 1970s, regularly hosting holistic and spiritual retreats (including an inaugural visit from spiritual leader Ram Dass).

The cabins are rustic, but they're thermally heated, so there is no need to worry about roughing it. Still, it helps to bring piles of cushy pillows and blankets to trick out your space. Vegetarian meals are included in the price and served up thrice daily in the community lodge that eschews caffeine and alcohol for citrus-mint lemonade and homemade pumpkin cookies.

While it's not necessarily a romance-focused space, couples will still find the forested grounds incredibly restorative and their hearts filled to the brim—whether they opt for on-site yoga, the clothing-optional springs, or a bird-watching hike (keep an eye out for bald eagles and chubby western tanagers).

More Fun

RAMONA FOREVER— This one takes some work, but boy is **Ramona Falls** worth it. Often name-dropped as one of the best hikes in Oregon, this seven-miler crescendos in a columnar basalt waterfall that is so grandiose it doesn't seem real.

POWER PLAY—An abandoned power plant at the base of the impressive **White River Falls** creates the backdrop for one of the most unique swimming holes in the state. Better yet, it's not uncommon for the sun to be shining on this side of the mountain when it's still gloomy in Portland.

TUBE THE LIGHT FANTASTIC—The sun sets disturbingly early in the winter, but Mount Hood Skibowl's **Cosmic Tubing** is there to help combat your seasonal affective disorder with a trippy alpine rave and live DJs. Grab a tube for two and fling yourself down the mountain surrounded by six hundred thousand LED lights, black lights, and lasers.

WHAT A BUTTE—Adventurous couples can sleep in this highly affordable one-room forty-foot-high **Fivemile Butte Lookout** fire tower, waking up in the heart of hiking country with views that just don't quit. But be warned, reservations for all of Oregon's lookout towers are notoriously cutthroat.

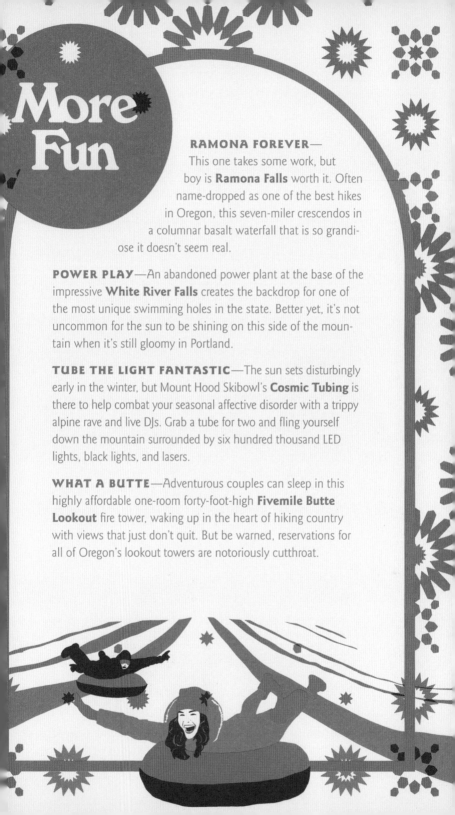

Willamette Valley

As Oregon's capital, Salem and its surrounding burgs form the central foundation for our state. It shares some admirable riverfront action with its Portland counterpart—the requisite parks, paths, and water-based activities—but only near the capitol will you find an adorably ancient amusement park, a sports fan's happy place, and a grand Fourth of July parade plucked right out of yesteryear.

SLANTED & ENCHANTED

In 1964, Roger Tofte bought twenty acres of forest just south of Salem and began sculpting fanciful cement characters to populate a storybook trail in the trees. Such was the beginning of **Enchanted Forest**, the sweetest psychedelic amusement park you'll ever visit. Harpsichord music (written by Tofte's daughter) fills the air while couples and families frolic and picnic in pockets along the various "neighborhoods" built out over the years. Steal a kiss next to the glowing blacklight waterfall deep in the Seven Dwarves House, squeal with joy as you're jammed in a log flying down a backwoods flume, or giggle at the janky (and sometimes terrifying) haunted

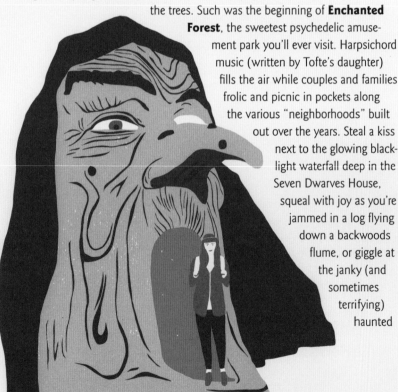

house animatronics. Let's be clear, even the knockoff Matterhorn roller coaster is best suited for nine-year-olds, but when you're crammed in that rocket car with your partner, getting tossed around like rag dolls on that creaky old track, age is only a construct. There is so much magic and love poured into every detail that it's impossible not to leave without being completely enamored by everything in this truly enchanted forest.

INDEPENDENCE DAY

Sure, lots of towns have celebrations for America's birthday, but few do it up like they do in **Independence, Oregon**. It's a whole day of celebrating 1776 in this bucolic and relatively unknown riverfront town. The day begins when the entire town comes out and lines Main Street for a grand parade that includes elderly Shriners zipping around in their little red cars, festive floats painstakingly decorated by local businesses, and the mayor ceremoniously following up the horse fleet with a shovel for the "gifts" left behind. Hop on

some carnival rides, check out the fair booths, and scarf down your weight in churros until sundown when **Riverview Park** alights with fireworks exploding over the Willamette, kiddos and grown-ups cheering in unison. 'Murica!

CAPITAL THRILL

Salem's connected waterfront parks make for a *Leave It to Beaver* level of pleasantness. Walking is good, but the real way to take advantage of this idyllic green space is to get yourself some wheels. We're talking bicycles, scooters, or even 1970s-era roller skates because there are miles and miles of wide paved paths forbidden to motor vehicles. Start at **Minto Brown Island Park** and cruise through twelve hundred acres of marshland and woods that double as a wildlife refuge. It's what Portland's Sauvie Island might be without the traffic. Whiz over the new **Peter Courtney Minto Island Bridge** to **Riverfront Park**, where you can take a gander at the old paper mill's acid storage ball turned **Eco-Earth Globe** art project, ogle the riverboat on the dock, and then be annoyingly cute by hopping on the fancy horsies (and llama!) and taking a spin on the **Riverfront Carousel**.

Lock up the bikes and grab a snack at **Archive Coffee & Bar**, a vintage/ industrial cafe with lots of leather books and a decadent bar in the center of the space. Speaking of decadence, order the Bee's Knees with espresso, cream, honey, rosemary, lavender, pepper, and sugar over ice. You've earned it. Before skipping town, pop into **Ranch Records**, which has kept the suburban kids cool as hell for four decades and counting. Their special Northwest grunge case will give you all the 1990s feels, but no matter your genre (or format) of choice, this ranch has you covered. It's a stand-up spot that could hold its own in any city, so throw them dollars down in support.

HOT TIP: Salem is known as the Cherry City, and in the spring, she really earns it. Go to the imposing capitol building for a spectacular cherry blossom walk along the promenade that leads up to the front doors. And don't stop there! We have one of the few open-door capitols, so take a look around and observe a chamber floor session while you're there. Couples who participate in democracy together, stay together.

EUGENE LOVEY

Farther south of Salem lies sports land. In Eugene, the University of Oregon's Ducks regularly battle the Oregon State Beavers in epic "Civil War" games dating back to 1894 that draw thousands of rabid admirers from all over the state. Hard-core visiting fans stay in the quack-themed **Graduate Eugene** hotel, where pre-funking is encouraged (as is a giant plate of post-game ravioli at **Beppe & Gianni's Trattoria**). The football team may be the first Ducks that come to mind, but don't forget about the school's *other* Ducks, namely the women's basketball team who are equally fun to watch and play indoors (no shivering games here!).

For the polar opposite experience, in July, visit our colorful **Oregon Country Fair**. Founded in 1969, this annual three-day festival is the epitome of what many folks think Oregon is. Held in the woods with most visitors camping for the duration, the nineteen stages are full of jugglers, magicians, and musicians swathed in tie-dye. Hundreds of artisans set up tables in an utterly unique pop-up show, complete with stained glass, tiny sculptures, and even trippy puppet people cruising around. There is no shortage of things to see at this fest.

Coast Range

The chain of mountains nestled between Portland and the sea is a dense and misty utopia exploding with lesser-known trails and fat edible mushrooms. The range spans the distance from our northern border down to the Coquille River. Bring your bike, try one of the non-touristy watering holes in an offbeat town, and screenshot those maps because GPS is spotty at best.

MAGIC MUSHROOMS

Come fall, a large percentage of Portlanders turn into real fun guys and trek to the **Tillamook Forest** in search of the elusive, delicious chanterelle mushroom. Though locals are exceedingly tight-lipped about their mushroom hunting spots, you can find your own with a few handy tips and bucketloads of patience. For the true beginner, it's as simple as noticing when your grocery store puts up a display of the golden 'shroom in the produce aisle. That means it's go time for a weekend adventure with a handy mushroom guidebook in hand, a sharp knife to cut them free, a gallon bucket, and a quick internet check on what the picking limit is for your area.

In general, you're looking for coniferous forests where the moss is dense and the forest floor is so thick it feels like walking on a shag carpet with your shoes off. Once your eyes adjust to the intricacies of the world below your feet, you'll notice entire empires of tiny 'shrooms and woodland wonders. Flit like pixies over toppled trees and through the brush, and after a while, it doesn't even matter if you stumble upon something edible. But if you do come across a gang of little chanti darlings poking their heads out of the needles, that feeling of triumph is unmatched. Both **Saddle Mountain** and **Kings Mountain** have alluring hikes with superb views from their peaks, so even if you don't find any foraged delicacies to take home, the day still provides fun.

Pat yourselves on the back or console your loss with some grub at **Camp 18**. The grounds double as a logging museum with farm kitties darting around massive band saws and tractor bits. Inside the roomy log cabin, a giant fireplace and antler chandeliers provide the appropriate backdrop for their hearty lumberjack fare.

KEEPIN' IT WHEEL

For one heck of a bicycle date, toss your rides in the back and head up to the **Banks-Vernonia State Trail**. Once a railroad bed with trains chugging along "I think I can" style, it's now twenty-one miles of easy(ish)-to-peddle paths. Alternate between slight climbs and coasts (though never too much, since it was all flattened out pretty well for the train tracks) across thirteen wooden trestle bridges, through flower-filled meadows in the summer, and beneath the vibrant canopy in the fall. Not up for the full trek? Access the trail at six different points to make this as short or long as you'd like.

If you get the chance, check out **Vernonia Open Air Market** every Saturday in the summer with its fresh farm eggs, homemade jams, and handmade crafts, culminating each year with the **Vernonia Salmon Festival**. Celebrate the return of the Chinook to the area and, if you're lucky, see those wild things making their way upstream in the adjoining Rock Creek.

Just outside town, the **abandoned Vernonia sawmill** is worth a visit but, if you can, keep the actual destination a surprise from your date. They'll think you're taking a short walk along the shores of Vernonia Lake, scouting graceful red-winged blackbirds and paddling ducks, but then you'll veer off to this rural curiosity. Covered floor to sky with graffiti murals ranging from Banksy wannabes to legit jaw-droppers, the roofless wonder—complete with trees growing up its core—is Oregon's most unexpected art gallery.

NORTH PLAINS
STATE OF MIND

Horning's Hideout is a popular party spot, hosting everything from creek-side weddings to raucous quinceañeras, but you don't need a milestone to take to the lake for a paddleboat race. If you're the faux-fishing type, the five-dollar

entrance fee also gets you poles and bait, and a stocked lake means you're almost guaranteed to get a nibble. And, for the Frolf inclined, this old-growth thicket hosts the Cadillac of disc golf courses with three distinct eighteen-hole options. Their Meadow Ridge course even got props in the industry as one of the best in the world.

Before you leave the North Plains area, you'll want to pay a visit to **Abbey Creek Winery**. Two seconds after setting foot inside, you'll find it's less stuffy than your typical tasting room. Hip-hop music blasts over the speakers, conversations are loud and lively, and you get the sense that everyone who walks through the door is a friend. Winemaker Bertony Faustin is usually on hand to entertain with stories about each of his cherished creations, offering tastes of chipotle hot sauce between sips. As one of only fifty Black winemakers in the world, and the first recorded in Oregon, he's prioritized bringing attention to other minority winemakers in the area by producing the documentary *Red, White & Black*, which addresses the challenges and success of winemakers of color, women, and the LGBTQ+ community. Buy a bottle from Faustin and imbibe at home while you watch and learn from one of the masters.

ZIPS & DIP

Get to know each other's terrified screams and gleeful squeals at **Tree to Tree Aerial Adventure Park**. You don't have to be a daredevil to enjoy the thrills this little Endor provides. Leap off a platform high in the trees and swish through the forest on a nearly quarter-mile-long zip line, or spend the afternoon navigating their self-guided aerial obstacle course with wobbly bridges, tightrope walks, and Tarzan swings.

All that pumping adrenaline can leave you with a sweaty glow. Cool off with a splash in neighboring **Hagg Lake**. The human-made lake has tons of nooks for a quick dip but not much in the way of sandy beaches, so think less lounging and more floating on an inflatable raft, dog-paddling,

or making friends with a boater kind of activities. The water's generally more tepid than most of the state's swimming holes, which makes up for the less-than-desirable muddy shoreline.

TREE HUGGERS

Only a handful of old-timers could tell you about the long-gone company town of Valsetz. A staple of the timber industry, its inhabitants lived remotely with their own post office deep in the forest. In 1983, due to dwindling old-growth timber, Boise Cascade announced they would cease operations and effectively tore down the entire town. All three hundred residents left, and the human-made Valsetz Lake was soon drained. Now only a whisper keeps its tale going.

You'll go right through the vanished township as you embark on this Seriously Advanced Level Adventure not for the faint of heart. The actual hike is only mildly difficult, it's the getting there that is exceedingly tricky. So why the hell do people do it? Because the five-hundred-year-old Douglas firs at the **Valley of the Giants** are so lovely and otherworldly, they bring an immediate sense of calm. It's the nature-viewing equivalent of taking a chill pill.

To get to this one-and-a-third-mile hike that travels over footbridges and scrambles over enormous tree roots, you must venture for miles in a series of complicated turns on unlabeled forest roads so remote the trees laugh in the face of your cell phone's GPS. Instead, a Bureau of Land Management brochure (available online) guides you out on the unpaved, unmarked single-lane roads where you might encounter an occasional logging truck barreling around the hairpin mountain turns. If you miss one of the *seventeen* directions with vague clues like "Continue on, passing through a rock quarry," you might wander lost for a while. Keep your cool, go slow, and when you finally get to the fallen "Big Guy," who is seven freaking feet in diameter, it'll feel extra dang special. You've surely seen some big trees in Oregon, but this secret grove is next level, or maybe it's just the effort it takes to find it. Let a loved one know your where-abouts before you leave and give yourself plenty of sunlight to make your way out of there, as the directions are even more befuddling in reverse.

North Coast

From the Victorian homes dotting the hills of Astoria to surfers carving the waves in Oswald West and a heap of oddball shops between, there is no shortage of sights on Oregon's northern coast. Whether you're a fiend for saltwater taffy or fresh-caught fish-and-chips, this part of the world is basically one big aphrodisiac.

SWEET ASTORIA

Astoria is what we'd describe as a quaint fishing village, but facts call it the first city in Oregon and the first permanent settlement west of the Rockies. It has a host of good things going for it, but it is of the utmost importance to Oregonians that everyone know *The Goonies* was filmed here. And we're never

letting that go.
Yes, it was made
many decades ago,
but "down here, it's
(still) our time!" The
iconic **Goonies House** is famously off-limits and often has tarps in front of
it (due to a curmudgeonly owner who likely was sick of kids doing the truffle
shuffle out his window 24/7) so you can only view it semi-obstructed from
afar, but don't worry, One-Eyed Willy has left plenty of other treasures for you
to discover.

Most of these can be found at **The Oregon Film Museum**, located in
the former county jail and immediately recognizable from the opening chase
scene from *The Goonies*. Inside, you can see artifacts from the other movies
Oregon proudly claims (like *One Flew Over the Cuckoo's Nest* and Arnold
Schwarzenegger's Oscar-worthy vehicle *Kindergarten Cop*). You and your
partner will never have as much fun as you'll have recreating scenes from *Point
Break* in front of a green screen. Just don't get into a fight over who gets to be
Keanu and who gets to be Swayze—they're both icons in our book.

Though its "Hollywood North" nickname might not be the first thing
that comes to mind, this old Nordic burg has lots to offer beyond film. Stop
into the **Street 14 Coffee** located in the bottom of the super cute/possibly
haunted **Commodore Hotel** for an Americano to go (in your own reusable
mug like a real Oregonian). Then, hand in hand, bop in and out of the fun
downtown shops. **Bach N' Rock Music** is a Swiss Army knife kind of record
shop, with a tea counter, a veritable jungle of plants, and chubby kitties
everywhere. Once vinyl is securely in hand, head to **Phog Bounders** for more

browsing fun. Fifty-five local antique dealers have booths for you to rummage through, and while the stock leans heavily on vintage nautical wares (glass buoy, anyone?), you're sure to find a keepsake for your retro shelf back home.

On the food front, options abound, but one requisite stop is an old dry-docked gill-net boat across from the **Columbia River Maritime Museum**. The **Bowpicker** serves up *one* dish from the windows of the vintage boat: beer-battered chunks of locally caught albacore tuna and thick fries. FYI, the line will be long, so come prepared with probing questions to pass the time. Equally important is the trifecta of the **Columbian Cafe**, **Voodoo Room**, and **Columbian Theater**. Connected on the same block, the teeny cafe—barely bigger than Grandma's kitchen—is great for brunch, while the quirky dive bar counterpart has stiff G&Ts and local bands in the evenings. Keep an eye on their calendar for Portland bands taking advantage of the intimate environment to perform special one-offs or warm-up shows outside their regular touring schedules.

PIERS FOR BEERS

Perched out on a pier, a refurbished fish cannery is now a fancy hotel with a day spa where you can soak and sauna while looking out at the long Astoria-Megler Bridge. In fact, one notable travel site declared the **Cannery Pier Hotel & Spa** one of the top twenty-five most romantic hotels in the country. Bow chicka wow wow. Big ol' boats go by your hotel room window, and nothing sets the mood like a crew of hot ~~seamen~~ sailors.

If you want to watch the sunset over the Pacific Ocean, it's worth the short trip down the road to Warrenton, where you can also view the **Peter Iredale shipwreck**, a steel barque from a fancy Liverpudlian that ran aground in 1906 and has been slowly deteriorating since. (Everyone on board survived, so it's not too goth to nuzzle.) Back in town, **Buoy Beer Co.** serves up the artichoke and hatch chile dip of your dreams in a revamped fish processing warehouse. Be sure to take note of their brilliant glass flooring through which you can witness chunky sea lions lounging and cavorting below.

YOU'VE GOT GAME

An important warning about Seaside, Oregon: do *not* take an uptight grump. This near circus—without the usual depressing animal captivity—is where you let your childish freak flag fly. We suggest starting with a walk along the 1920s-era promenade and further sightseeing by land or water via tandem bicycles or ginormous swan paddleboats (swoon!), both available from **Wheel Fun Rentals**.

Now that you've got the lay of the land, it's time to hatch a plan of attack. Cool your burning thighs by pulling up a stool at **Bridge Tender** tavern and ordering a frosty adult treat. This riverside shanty with its well-worn billiards tables is a great place to get your competitive impulses warmed up.

Are you feeling like a baller yet? Because it's about to get real. Among the dinging bells and

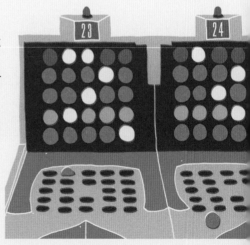

sugar-hyped children squealing at the **Funland Entertainment Center** lies a secret haven—the room of **Fascination**. Grab a seat at one of the many table-top alleys, plunk down a whole quarter, and "at the sound of the bell . . . roll 'em!" Like a cross between bingo and bowling with an unruly rubber ball, this addictive game pits you against everyone else in the room as you race to be the first to sink a line of five balls in a row. There's always a winner and since there's little skill involved there's a good chance, at some point, it will be you. It requires zero thought and is rounds and rounds of addictive fun. Trade your winning tickets for a set of dominoes to take back to wherever you're staying and, after getting hopped up on sugar-crusted elephant ears, saltwater taffy, and soft-serve ice cream, let the games continue.

ONE-NIGHT SAND

Arguably Oregon's fanciest beach town, **Cannon Beach** delivers everything you want from a classic beach day, namely soft sand and excellent views. *Nat Geo* once included it in the top one hundred most beautiful places on earth! NBD. Aside from the scenic Haystack Rock (one of several Haystack Rocks in the state) and the nostalgic main street—made for primo strolling, with ice-cream shops, breweries, and boutiques—every June, this town dials up the whimsy even fur-ther. We're talking **Cannon Beach Sandcastle Contest**, where everyone from newbies to professionals are welcome. So polyamorous peeps and type A folks, call upon your superior scheduling skills to gather the whole gang because this is an all-hands-on-deck situation. Once the judges have anointed the victor, the festivities continue with a giant beach bonfire and live music. It's about as Frankie and Annette as you can get in this part of the world.

BEACH BOPPING

Time to get out of your dreams and into your car. Check your tide tables and drive to **Hug Point State Park** when it's low-ish tide or you'll be treading water. Ditch the shoes and meander north to see where pioneers had to hug their stagecoaches against the sandstone before roads were built here. This short walk will gift you with a waterfall that trickles in summer and gushes in winter but always proffers a good excuse to sneak a hug.

Two miles farther down the road, **Oswald West State Park** is the Cadillac of beach parks. You wanna hike a mountain? Scramble through old-growth forests to the summit of Neah-Kah-Nie Mountain for a view that goes on forever, or choose the half-mile walk down the hill to **Short Sands** to watch the surfers. (Yes, Oregon has them, but their wet suits are very, very *thick*.) This lavish nook is named after one-term governor Oswald West, a Progressive reformer who believed all of Oregon's beaches should be declared a public highway, thus ensuring every inch of our beautiful coast belongs to *all*. Or as he more eloquently said upon leaving office in 1915, "No selfish interest should be permitted, through politics or otherwise, to destroy or even impair this great birthright of our people." *Thanks, Ozzy!!!*

HOT TIP: Oregon beaches allow small fires that come with a few completely reasonable rules. Educate yourself, then spark some romance by showing off your mastery of the original tinder.

HOT DATE ON A STICK

Picturesque Wheeler, just a bit farther south, sits inland from the coastline along Nehalem Bay. This small railroad stop of a town might feel far removed from city life, but its **Salmonberry Saloon** has deep Portland roots. Helmed by Chantelle Hylton—booker for beloved but no-longer-with-us Portland music venues The Blackbird and Berbati's Pan—and her Wheeler-raised partner, Patrick Rock, this delightful spot ups the ante on coastal cuisine and modern cocktail concoctions. Arrive hungry and ready to make some new friends. Before you leave town, hop across the main drag to check out **Wheeler Station Antiques**, which looks like a small mom-and-pop shop from the outside, but inside, it somehow unfolds for miles, chock-full of every vintage item under the sun.

Even if you're still full, dive into a bit of deep-fried history (or a quick ride on what we can only assume is the world's only mechanical corn dog) at **Pronto Pup** in Rockaway Beach. It was here, in the 1930s, where married duo Versa and George Boyington invented the corn dog as a way to not have the rain ruin the buns in their beachside hot-dog stand. Not all heroes wear capes.

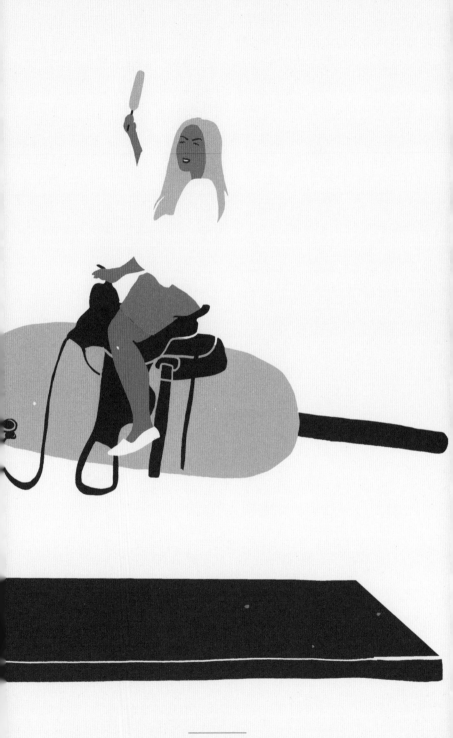

ZONE 5

A Real Commitment

Long Beach 5

• MT. RAINIER

12

Volcanoes

• MT. ST. HELENS

97

• ASTORIA

30

84

PENDLETON

• PORTLAND

Journey
Through
Time

26

395

Mid-Coast

• NEWPORT

20

High
Desert

26

JOHN DAY

126

• BEND

58

97

20

Land of
Lakes

01

5

CRATER LAKE

395

90

Volcanoes

The Pacific Northwest is a hotbed for volcanoes. In Oregon, many of Mount Hood's best offerings revolve around winter funtivities, but in Washington, summertime reigns for both Rainier and St. Helens. Once the adverse weather conditions clear, take advantage of their globally admired wildflowers, jaw-dropping scenic drives, and wild (and weird) trails.

TWO TICKETS TO PARADISE

Mount Rainier, a stratovolcano who does as she pleases, has endless dates with all the trails, views, and wildlife. Get on **The Road to Paradise**, which is not our attempt at innuendo but the actual can't-miss circuitous route up the south slope rife with heart-stopping views. Once you hit the aptly named Paradise area, take a break for lunch at the **Paradise Inn**, a handsome old lodge with massive exposed cedar logs and a towering grandfather clock. Then hop onto the **Nisqually Vista Trail** for what some folks swear hosts the best explosion of wildflowers anywhere in the world. Colorful splashes of magenta Indian paintbrush, sunny yellow monkey flowers, and happy purple lupine-saturated meadows with thousands of flowers (plus larkspur, shooting stars, lilies, and so many more) make it seem as if a rainbow exploded onto this plot of earth.

To maximize your time in the area, you may want to consider hunkering down for a night or two. Three miles away from

Rainer's southwest entrance lies **Wellspring Spa and Woodland Retreat**. The sprawling grounds resemble an adorable elfin village with overgrown gardens, a stone labyrinth, communal firepits everywhere, and a cluster of cabins ranging from ramshackle to bam(!)shackle. Opt for one of the newer builds, with soaring log ceilings, a reading loft with a napping hammock, and gorgeous river-rock fireplace, and forgo the additional hot-tub fee because your cabin comes with a jetted heart-shaped soaking tub right in the main room. Go for long walks in the forest, read aloud to each other, and get super chill. This Wi-Fi-free, cell-service-free spot is for enjoying nature (and each other).

Though the cabins come with kitchens, it's worth a venture out to try the local cuisine or take a break from cooking. At **Copper Creek Inn**, devour sandwiches on thick-sliced homemade bread and lust-worthy pies inside this storied local haunt. The wall mural of deer grazing before an alpine lake at the base of a snowy Rainier was painted by a neighbor but could definitely be in a hip art show. And don't leave the area without a visit to the seasonally open **Wildberry Restaurant**. Owned by Lhakpa Gelu Sherpa, who not only holds the world speed record for Mount Everest by hitting the summit in just under eleven hours, he's climbed the dang thing fifteen times! For half the year, his wife, Fulamu, serves up both typical American grub and Himalayan specialties, then they close to tend to their other restaurant in Kharikhola, Nepal.

HOT TIP: Since the 1970s, Packwood's four-day annual Labor Day Flea Market is a scene and then some. Thousands of visitors flock to the small town to comb through tent after tent of crafts, antiques, dishware, old birdhouses, and other oddities.

HAVE A BLAST

Pull a Kenny Loggins and ride into the danger zone at **Windy Ridge**, the heart of the Mount St. Helens blast area. It's a trip to see where the earth just lost her cool and exploded everywhere, leveling everything in its wake in a matter of seconds. As you drive up the winding switchback road, you'll see the full extent of destruction from the 1980 eruption as the magnificent forest of green morphs into a cemetery of dead trees, and then into an ashy nothingness.

Once you make it to the ridge, schlep to the very top for a view into the crater and out over log-clogged Spirit Lake.

On the other side of the park, witness more feats of hot magma action with a day of educational exploration at the surely Bill Nye–approved trifecta of Trail of Two Forests, Ape Caves, and Lava Canyon. Each of the distinct spots has its own personality and level of difficulty. (Side note: Check out the US Forest Service's YouTube series *Accessible Adventures in the Pacific Northwest* for enlightening first-person accounts on experiencing this region via wheelchair.)

At **Trail of Two Forests**, roam through both an old-growth forest and one forever changed by the blast. Here, you'll find lava casts—three-dimensional imprints of trees in the old lava bed—including one you can descend eight feet into via a ladder. Additional spelunking-esque activities are mere minutes away at the much larger **Ape Cave Lava Tube**. At two and a half miles long, this is one of the longest lava tubes in the world, formed from a previous eruption some two thousand years ago. This is a pitch-black hike that requires light sources, warm layers, and zero claustrophobia. Finally, have one last blast with a hike through **Lava Canyon**, which is jam-packed with all kinds of Indiana Jones–style activities. Cliffside ladders! Bouncy suspension bridges! Temples of doom (OK, not this one)! This is one of the most spectacular hikes around, but it can also be extremely dangerous, and sections of the trail have closed and reopened over the years. Just be like Indy and use your smarts out there.

Journey Through Time

This epic scenic byway is a master class in Oregon history, but one that's far more fun than sitting in a lecture hall. The eastern part of our state offers something entirely different than the rainy forests and bustling cities of the west. Explore remnants of pioneer days, numerous (and definitely haunted) old buildings, the most beautiful geology conceivable, and all the complex human history that comes along with any sort of journey through time.

WILD WILD COUNTRY

Head east from Portland on I-84 through the gorgeous Gorge (heavily covered on page 74), until you coast into The Dalles. Fuel up for the long day ahead with a visit to **Spooky's** pizza parlor. Originally opened in 1966 but forever trapped in the 1980s, you're likely to hear Hall and Oates kick out the jams while flaunting your arcade skills. This isn't the wood-fired, arugula-topped pie of modern times; this is the classic cornmeal-crust pizza of yesteryear, and it's still as lip smacking as ever.

This journey is all about going back in time. To that end, check out the flashing neon lights of Broadway, Route 66, and the original Las Vegas strip. Specimens from all these places and more are gathered at the **National Neon**

Sign Museum. Yes, it's a niche-as-hell date, but on display is the literal first-ever neon light tube by French inventor George Claude. Being this close to history will light up even the dark hearted. You'll never look at Portland's iconic White Stag sign the same.

Even further back in time, you'll find the charming ghost town of **Shaniko**. Surrounded by sagebrush, and with its most recent census population coming in at a whopping thirty-six, this was once the "Wool Capital of the World." Today it might be a contender for one of the more Instagrammable spots in the world. Grab an ice-cream cone from one of the only functioning shops and walk the rickety old wooden sidewalks, snapping as many double selfies as possible.

From here, you'll turn onto Highway 97, the beginning of the actual **Journey Through Time Scenic Byway**, a designated highway that fully lives up to its name. To truly appreciate this part of the world in full, it is of the utmost importance that you have done your homework before you arrive. To be more specific, the week before you set out on this passage, embark on a Netflix (sans chill, just this once) pre-adventure by taking in the docuseries *Wild Wild Country*. The episodes will walk you through the outrageous tale of Bhagwan Shree Rajneesh/Osho and his right-hand woman, Ma Anand Sheela, who relocated from India to this unincorporated vast area of Oregon and took it over with thousands of cultish followers in tow. And gurrrrrllllllll was it messy. Depending which Oregonian you ask, you might get an earful about powerful Portlanders shopping at Nordstrom to pick up the requisite red fashions that Bhagwan's followers, the Rajneeshees, wore. Or you might hear about the entire new city they built out in the desert while battling with the locals, the

purposeful poisonings of Oregonians, the hotel bombings, the massive fleet of Rolls-Royces, or the political assassination plots. Yeah, *mes-sy*. The commemorative plaque outside the **Antelope Post Office** doesn't do the incredibly layered story justice, so binge the short series for maximum backstory.

But 1980s cults are so over, so best to jet down the road to the **Clarno Unit** for a fantasy fortress courtesy of nature. Created a kazillion years ago by massive landslides that splashed up land into the shapes of jagged turrets, the Palisades are a near regal sight. Take the easy quarter-mile trail to see some of the almost two hundred species of ancient nuts, fruits, and seeds that the tiny four-toed horses of the time scarfed up in a surely adorable manner. Stick the landing on your day of epic landscapes by pulling up to the genuinely jaw-dropping crimson, rust, and ochre stripes of the **Painted Hills** in the golden light of the late afternoon. A unit within the **John Day Fossil Beds National Monument**— and declared one of the Seven Wonders of Oregon—these magic mounds are a top-notch romance spot. If you don't hold hands while walking the millions of years of colorful natural history here, you're doing it wrong.

SPUR OF THE MOMENT

You're probably familiar with the iconic patterns of **Pendleton Woolen Mills** blankets and fabric established back in 1863 or with the world-famous **Pendleton Round-Up** rodeo that's brought all the boys to the yard for over a century. Pendleton is an Old West town that acknowledges its deeply upsetting first years (see America/Racism/1800s for *way too many* examples) and lets you tour the town's illegal gambling sites, brothels, and underground tunnels.

This town may look similar to what it looked like 170 years ago with its tall and lean historic brick buildings and fancy facades, but it's getting hip to the times. The **Pendleton Farmers Market** (Friday evenings from spring until fall) showcases more artisan goods and talented crafters than one might expect this far from any major metropolis. At **Old School Shirt Makers New York**, also on the main drag but open year-round, find co-owner Kevin Stewart—former fashion director at ESPN—dapperly dressed with an ascot slightly askew. He and his life/work partner, Kay Davis, have racks of modern Western shirts made of patterned cotton and

fancy snap buttons that are defining the next generation of style for this celebrated city.

Spend the evening just like the cowboys of the Old West with some good old-fashioned saloon hopping. Ease into things at the **Great Pacific**, a slightly newer joint, which often hosts live music by Portland luminaries (check out posters for Dave Depper and Nick Jaina on the walls). Though the décor is made up of twinkly lights and those nouveau-hippie paper star lanterns, the lively vibe is pure country charm.

A quick stroll down the block reveals the straight-up bordello vibes of **Virgil's at Cimmiyotti's**. Blood-red flocked velvet wallpaper, crystal chandeliers, stained glass, and a lot of pictures of old cattle ranchers adorn the room, while old cattle ranchers eating steaks fill the room. Meta. Belly up to the bar, choose your poison, and take it all in. You ain't in Portland anymore.

Round the night out at the **Rainbow Cafe**, a neon-lit diner that can bring out a gloriously diverse crowd of rowdy locals that defies the stereotypes of a small cowboy town. It's a fun scene where goth kids dance alongside gray-haired hippies, and everyone is welcome. After all the partying, sleep soundly at the incredibly affordable **Working Girls Hotel**, a former brothel that definitely has history/friendly ghosts roaming its lovely Victorian hallways.

FOSSIL FOOLS

"Life, uh, finds a way" on this special history day that begins with an ancient pharmacy and ends in a likely Jeff Goldblum–approved dinosaur date. Before we go back 55 million years, let's take one last pit stop in 1885. After "mysterious" fires wiped out various Chinese settlements in Eastern Oregon (again, see America/Racism/1800s), many of the displaced immigrants moved to John Day, making its Chinatown the third largest in the country behind only San Francisco and Portland. Two men, "Doc" Ing Hay and Lung On, ran a multifaceted business, **Kam Wah Chung**, which was part mercantile, part boarding house, part religious center for other Buddhists, and the area's largest pharmacy, serving both the Chinese and White population (a big freaking deal at the time).

Doc Hay was famous throughout the region for being able to cure ailments that stumped traditional Western doctors through his extensive apothecary of things like cicada shells, white peony leaves, and slithering snakes in jars. He grew such a reputation in his sixty years of practice that people would send letters from all over describing their symptoms and asking him to send medicines back in the post. When he fell and broke his hip in 1948, the doors of Kam Wah Chung closed suddenly, perfectly preserving everything inside for decades. You can take free guided tours of the historic space, that is now a state park, complete with Doc Hay's undisturbed shelves of herbs and artifacts so intact it's known as one of the top-three preserved apothecaries in the world. Due to its size, only eight visitors are allowed in each hour, so plan accordingly.

Hop back on the **JTT Scenic Byway**, where it's not just possible but highly likely you'll see a massive skeleton creepily sprawled out on the side of the road like a modern-day fossil. Up to a quarter of the state is devoted to the study of genuine fossil activity, and the **Thomas Condon Paleontology and Visitor Center** in the **Sheep Rock Unit** is all about it. View paleontologists picking at bones in their fishbowl work center, see colorful murals with illustrations of what this land looked like in different eras, and be wowed by fantastically detailed fossils of creatures you never even knew roamed the area. Did you know at one point Oregon was a tropical climate that had *no winter*? You'll learn more than you ever did in school, and the public bathrooms are A+, which is always a dream while road-tripping.

If fabricated dioramas aren't your thing, you can see some of these artifacts out in the real world by taking the easy one-and-a-half-mile **Island in Time Trail** in the **Blue Basin** where you'll come across fossils frozen for all eternity in their natural habitat, including a massive tortoise who met an untimely end on these surreal blue cliffs, and the remains of long-gone animals like an oreodont sheep creature and a Nimravus giant cat. Unreal. But totes real.

High Desert

We get a bad rap in Oregon for being a land of never-ending rain, but the leaky sky is actually quarantined to the left side of the map. Nearly a quarter of the state is high desert with three hundred days of sunshine a year and an infinite number of outdoor activities, thanks to the wealth of rivers, lakes, and other geological wonders in the area.

DESERT COURSE

Prepare for your desert adventures by packing up that ride with *all* the extras, darling. We're talking water shoes, sunscreen, bug spray, layers upon layers, towels, reusable water bottles, 1,001 remixes of "Old Town Road," and a stash of granola bars to prevent any possible date-downer hanger attacks. Take Highway 26 over the mountain and through the Warm Springs Reservation. Keep an eye out for wild horses roaming through the sage—some with lazy stowaway birdies atop their spotted backs—as you cruise toward your first pit stop. (Side note: If one of you doesn't yell "Horses!" and point every time they come into view, please search your souls.) As you near the three-hour driving

SMITH
ROCK
STATE
PARK

mark, you'll come across the state's best place to pee *and* have a romantic walk: **Peter Skene Ogden State Scenic Viewpoint**.

Besides the requisite bathrooms, picnic tables, and leg-stretching grounds, a short stroll will lead you to a pedestrian bridge three hundred feet above the Crooked River Canyon and a view of the marvelous **Crooked River High Bridge**, which was the second-highest railroad bridge in the country when it was built in 1911. History plaques abound—take them all in before heading a few miles down the road to rock-climbing heaven **Smith Rock**.

Offering two thousand climbing routes and known colloquially as the birthplace of modern rock climbing, the 650-acre park is what we like to call "peak outdoors." The less gutsy among us will find horseback and mountain biking paths as well as the two-and-a-half-mile **River Trail**, popular with novices, doggos, and families. It circles a good amount of the park with a mostly flat trail and a stellar view of the iconic 350-foot spire **Monkey Face**, where you might spy climbers dangling from its smiling face or slackliners providing major circus vibes. All this for a measly five-dollar parking permit. #worthit

After you've worked up that appetite (and believe us, you will) drive just another half hour into Bend, a haven of breweries, skiers, and lazy river rafters. Inside the supes-cutes **Old Town Historic District** chockablock full of quaint Craftsman-style homes, you'll find **Jackson's Corner**. The house turned restaurant has an on-site bakery with daily baguettes and tangy sourdoughs as well as naturally leavened pizza dough topped with ingredients from neighboring farms.

AROUND THE BEND

OCEAN
- ROLL -

4 35

Come morning in Bend, stop by Scott Street for the ultra-adorable **Sparrow Bakery** located in the city's Old Ironworks Art District, where everything from the ivy-clad crumbling brick to the breezy patio is a delight. Make sure to try their signature Ocean Roll made from croissant dough and stuffed with cardamom-vanilla sugar.

As the caffeine begins to soak into the bloodstream, the River Fun Times™ are about to begin! The city takes the art of lazily floating in water to a new level with their **Bend Park & Float** program.

From June until September, find everything from inner tube rentals to changing stations to a shuttle service that will take you and your hottie with a body to the top of the white-water park. There, it's choose-your-own-adventure time. There's the **Fish Ladder** (picture a determined little salmon trying to climb a ladder) with a couple of baby rapids, perfect for kiddos and mellow peeps. The **Whitewater Channel** is for people who like to make waves. Literally. It has four wave features for kayakers, paddleboarders, and surfers who know how to handle their white water.

You'll be hungry and sleepy after spending hours appreciating the majesty of the Deschutes in the happy sunshine. Before heading out, clean up all your trash. (For reals on this, there's been a problem with horrible humans leaving behind garbage, and you don't want to be a horrible human!) Now, you get to live like Cher and turn back time with a stop at the **Pilot Butte Drive-In** restaurant. A former A&W, it became a local burgers-and-shakes joint in 1983 and has maintained its popularity thanks to its old-school car orders, mountainous burgers (plus one Gardenburger option for the vegheads), and crispy fries. Over-order, grab the ketchup, and congratulate each other on your athletic water skillz.

GET YOUR ROCKS OFF

The town of Sisters isn't named such for being the little sibling of Bend but for the three peaks poking up behind it: **North Sister**, **Middle Sister**, and **South Sister**. Take advantage of the sunny side of the ridge on the spacious tiered patio of the **Depot Cafe**. Tables are far enough apart to spill all the juicy personal info while devouring omelets and pancakes among hosta-filled barrels and overflowing petunia baskets.

Post-brunch, steal away for one of the weirder roadside attractions this state has to offer. And we mean that in the absolute best way. Built by Danish immigrant Rasmus Petersen from 1935 until his death in 1952, the slowly decaying **Petersen Rock Garden** has been a popular roadside attraction for many years and, in 2013, was added to the National Register of Historic Places. Slip six dollars cash into the donation box and take in the seemingly millions of mounds of jasper, malachite, obsidian, and agate carefully sculpted into replicas of castles, bridges, and even the Statue of Liberty. The four acres—complete with beautiful roaming peacocks—include plenty of benches to sit and listen to croaking frogs or marvel at flourishing pink lily pads. Inside the tiny rock

SOUVENIRS AND CURIOS
FLUORESCENT MINERAL DISPLAY

RAREST STONES
DISPLAYED IN MUSEUM

Redmon

Petersen
Rock Garden

Old Redmond Highway

Highway 97

Oregon's
Famous
PETERSEN'S
Rock Garden
COLORFUL SPECTACLE OF MAN'S HANDIWORK
Between Bend and Redmond

SEE ROCKS FROM WAY OUT!

"museum," view massive thunder eggs and chat with Petersen's kin about geological wonders or ornery Shetland ponies. The place may be decomposing under the desert sun, but this only adds to the charm.

Back in Sisters, spend some time meandering the main drag with its 1880s facades. The artsy community has all kinds of antique shops, bookstores, and sugar opportunities. If it's not the dead of winter, make sure to stop into **Richard's Farmstand** for seriously yum seasonal produce like tart Bing cherries and fat, drippy marionberries. If you haven't killed your appetite with all the snacking, art gallery/wine bar **The Open Door** (reservations usually required) is a sweet spot for dinner. With any luck, you'll be seated in the darling white greenhouse made from antique windows in their roomy courtyard.

SUTTLE SIGNALS

The beauty of **Suttle Lake** comes to us courtesy of a typo. John Settle "discovered" (because, you know, Native people already lived here) the lake on a hunting trip in 1866, but thanks to some shoddy copyediting, "Settle" became "Suttle." Regardless, this lake and its accompanying lodge are worth a visit. **The Suttle Lodge** comes from some of the peeps behind Portland's Ace Hotel, and the food menu for their boathouse was designed by Joshua McFadden of Ava Gene's and Tusk fame. If your pocketbook doesn't allow for one of the spendier lodge rooms, book a plumbing-free rustic cabin, or just snag an ultra-cheap first-come-first-served camping spot at one of three nearby campgrounds and wander over to explore. You don't need to be a guest of the lodge to just hang.

In addition to pricey food and great drinks, the **Boathouse** offers rentals for romantic canoeing (as long as you don't tip over) and mountain bikes. A pleasant lakeside path will lead you to an abandoned women's restroom with Miss Havisham ambiance and a working piano made of branches. Serenade your love while they add your names to the wall alongside "Ruthie + Jason," "Matty + David," and the "Cuddle up club." In the great room of the lodge, a bar serves up drinks and pizzas while records from Death Cab for Cutie to David Bowie beg to be spun on the communal turntable. Outside, guests in Adirondacks gaze at the sunset glittering on the lake. A summer series brings in bands on the main lawn, allowing hipster babies and their tattooed parents to rock out together under the old-growth pines.

More Fun

LET'S GET LOST—Each spring, **Lost Lake** drains down a mysterious tube and turns into a grassy meadow by summer.

LOOKING FOR MR. WRIGHT—Sure, sure. Stunner views like this are abundant in the Cascades, but the alien landscape and ramshackle caveman architecture of the **Dee Wright Observatory** make it a must-stop when crossing the McKenzie Pass.

CARE TO DANCE—OUT Central Oregon regularly updates their website with LGBTQ+ events in the area, including a quarterly **Queer Dance Night**.

PLAYING HOUSE—Spend a weekend on the water with a rental from **Lake Billy Chinook Houseboats**. It ain't cheap but it is unforgettable, and for every extra friend you invite, the price could be reduced exponentially.

POWER COUPLE—Removed from the sprawling private estate known as **House on Metolius**, and perched atop a sparkling spring, the tiny **Power House** provides a luxurious weekend getaway (as in away from literally everything).

Land of Lakes

The barren landscape south of Bend is dotted with uncrowded swimming holes all the way to the California border. This Land of Lakes encompasses a historic scenic byway (labeled one of the top ten in the country) that was once paved with red volcanic cinders from the region and includes the state's longest lava tube cave and America's deepest lake. If you're into volcanoes inside of lakes inside of volcanoes—and really, who wouldn't be—you'll want to start packing your weekender bag pronto.

SWIM PICKINS

It is a fact that scenic drives are sexy. That means, scientifically speaking, of course, that the sixty-six-mile **Cascade Lakes Scenic Byway**—full of fourteen picturesque alpine lakes, towering pines, and volcanic rock strata—is nearly X-rated. For the physically adventurous, this strip also offers everything from mountain biking and fishing opportunities to snowshoeing and canoeing.

Drive along the winding road and pop in and out of nature heaven whenever the mood strikes. At **Sparks Lake**, admire the colorful paddleboards zipping across the lake as **Mount Bachelor** and **South Sister** come into the view, or try **Twin Lakes**, which has been such a longtime popular fishing spot that President Hoover even had a cabin on-site. Though, for the record, not

our favorite president (see negative views on Civil Rights and positive views on Prohibition). At **Elk Lake**, make the group date of your dreams come true by renting out their floating dock for the day. It comes with a BBQ, hammock, changing rooms, ample seating, and a ladder to climb back up after gleefully cannonballing into the frosty waters.

LAVA AT FIRST SIGHT

Steel yourselves, because the Lava Times™ are about to begin! Thanks to some real pissed-off volcanoes a few million years ago, you get to have a helluva day. At the **Lava River Cave**, descend fifty-five steps below the earth to explore the longest lava tube in the state. Pack a flashlight for this mini spelunking experience—the two-and-a-quarter-mile round-trip hike gets darker and darker as you crawl over planks and stairs into the always 42°F bat-filled cave. It's more cool than creepy, we promise.

Once you've returned from your journey to the center of the earth, set your sights on the moon. Sort of. The Rhode Island–size **Newberry National Volcanic Monument** (which was almost a national park before losing out to Crater Lake) is so similar to a lunar landscape that NASA sent astronauts here to bounce around in preparation for the moon landing. Apollo 15 astronaut James Irwin even left a little piece of lava from the area on the surface of the moon in 1971. So I guess you can say Oregon is officially out of this world. (We'll be here all night, folks. JUST LIKE THE MOON.)

But how is this all here? After a massive eruption, the volcano collapsed, leaving a crater filled with not one but two popular lakes in addition to stunning lava flows full of volcanic glass that are essentially lunar mimes. Follow the **Big Obsidian Flow Trail** to see more of the shiny black rock while fully nerding out on the thought of Neil Armstrong and Buzz Aldrin perfecting the *literal* moonwalk.

To keep on theme, pack an insulated tote stocked with moon pies, rocket pops, or freeze-dried astronaut ice-cream packets to complement your perfect alfresco feast. We suggest hitting the side-by-side **Paulina Falls**, just steps from the parking lot, whose eighty-foot plunge makes for a low-effort, high-reward picnic spot.

CRATER DATE

About 7,700 years ago, Mount Mazama blew its top and created **Crater Lake**, the deepest lake in the United States. The great depth absorbs red light rays, meaning the waters are bluer than Chris Pine's eyes. It's one of Oregon's Seven Wonders, and you'll drive through old-growth forests before arriving at the crater's edge and the two-thousand-foot-high cliffs that look down on the placid azure water, complete with the magical **Wizard Island** nestled in the middle. Now this is what we call a *viewing* lake, as opposed to a swimming lake, due to the cliffs sitch and the freezing water (though there is one section where you can attempt a dip). But the view is worth it, and the history plaques dotting the landscape are all equally worth the time.

You can go the traditional route by driving the rim and hopping in and out to scamper up rocks and mini trails, or take the snuggle option of climbing into one of the adorbs trolleys for a two-hour open-air sightseeing tour. Athletic peeps would be well advised to attend one of the twice-yearly vehicle-free days, when bikes flood the twenty-four-mile road. Afterward, stop into the **Crater Lake Lodge**—known for its test-your-patience-level service— to nab a decent martini, settle into a rough-hewn chair on the patio, and gaze at nature's fine work.

LIFE IS BUT A DREAM

Close your eyes and imagine the world's most romantic date. Did a rowboat
pop into your mind? Let's face it, that's about as basic as a candlelit dinner or a
bed strewn with rose petals. But plop that boat into a crystalline lake and stick
a still-standing three-thousand-year-old forest under the water, and you've got
some next-level titillation right there. **Clear Lake** is formed from snow runoff
that filters through caverns for twenty years. Icy temps reduce the number of
organisms that might otherwise muck up a lake, effectively preserving a stand
of trees that dates back to the basin's volcanic inception. The resort's customer
service leaves much to be desired, but rent a boat and serenely float over this
otherworldly dreamscape.

FAR & AWAY

For adventurous drivers wanting to push on in search of lesser traveled roads,
the many hours of podcast listening will be rewarded grandly. Try ogling the
aptly named two-mile fissure **Crack in the Ground** from both above and
within. Out in Silver Lake, the **Cowboy Dinner Tree** looks straight up like
an old west movie set serving up the same beans and biscuits from their
saddle-laden cabin that cowboys have eaten on the trail for generations. At
Fort Rock Caves, an architectural dig unearthed some of the oldest human
evidence in North America with several 9,000- to 11,000-year-old sagebrush
sandals (surely fly AF in their day). And if your stamina can withstand, **The
Outback Scenic Byway** is the antithesis of what most people think Oregon
looks like: expansive plains, flat desert landscapes, and an estimated forty-three
hundred wild horses running free like the cover of a dime store romance novel.

Mid-Coast

There are no big cities on Oregon's coast, but the string of small towns along Highway 101 are teeming with charm. Visit sleepy sea lions lounging on docks, climb to see the fantastic views from historic lighthouses, or maybe become an expert kite flier.

MOONRISE KINGDOM

If you eat cheese, you know Tillamook, the North Star of cheddar. But might we suggest a simple wave to the behemoth of factories as you travel to the far less crowded, petting-zoo-having, cheese-sample-flowing alternative **Blue Heron French Cheese Company** for your dairy fix? Cheesy things not your style? Alternative option is the **Hidden Acres Greenhouse & Café** with giant dinosaur-style plants, hydrangeas bigger than a human head (which weighs eight pounds—thank you, *Jerry Maguire*), and mighty hanging baskets for sale that'd make any neighbor jealous. Inside, you will find some trinkets that are definitely Grandma approved and a tiny cafe serving light salads and wraps.

But the most romantic of romantic to-dos comes at dusk when you climb into your little vessel for a moonlit paddle on the bay with **Kayak Tillamook**. As the sun goes down and the croaking frogs come out, row up to floating water lilies and around beaver dams. Pack some raver-style glow-in-the-dark bracelets to crack, activate, and slap on your wrists and oars. Continue on under the stars, tracking your lover by the neon bits moving over the calm water. This one is real special, so save it for someone who deserves it.

THE WORLD IS
YOUR OYSTER

Get lit first thing in the morning . . . with a trip to **Cape Meares Lighthouse**.
Once you park on the dramatic cliffside peak, take the five-minute mini hike
to see a tree unlike any other. Officially, it's a Sitka spruce, but really it's the
Octopus Tree. A giant one-hundred-foot version of Ursula sitting on the
coast for three hundred years with mysterious origins. She's gorgeous. Wander
around the paths from the lighthouse and climb it to see the fancy Fresnel lens.
It's a primo location for spotting whales traveling to and fro from Alaska in
March, April, December, and January, and for shrieking, "Thar she blows!"

The mini town of Oceanside has a fun secret. Not only does the soft sand
beach with particularly friendly seabirds make for serious sand naps, a tower
of rocks at the north end of the beach hides a tunnel. Take a kite and climb
through to the secret **Tunnel Beach** only accessible via the hobbit hole. Toss
that kite in the air and feel the breeze with the other members of the cool kids'
club. No secret handshake required.

Depending on the time of day, you can grab a late brekky nearby at the
Blue Agate Café, where the wait time for the fresh French toast and biscuits
can be long but worth it. Or if you're leaning toward dinner, try **The Schooner**
at Netarts Bay; its big ol' patio is protected but airy, thanks to partial glass walls.
You like oysters? They come right from this bish. Like right here. Like the chef
went out and dug them up after you ordered them.

If you can stay calm enough to navigate the Myspace-era website, book
one of the simple little cabins at **Cape Lookout**: they overlook the ocean, have
access to camp BBQs and trails, and feature too many giant trees to count.

COME FLY WITH ME

Every June and October, the **Lincoln City Kite Festival** turns the beach
into a childhood dream. Giant blue whales, rainbow stingrays, and tabby cats
the size of blimps float and sway in the wind while teams of expert fliers do
choreographed numbers with their stunt kites to such hits as Montell Jordan's
"This Is How We Do It." It's all free and pretty dang fun.

After the dreamy day of flying high, pop up to Pacific City to climb the
butt-bustin' dune and take in the massiveness of Haystack Rock. Admire the
longboard surfers who hang out on the break and roll their station wagon–length

rides into shore. Each fall, there's even a longboard competition ideal for land-lubbing spectators. Toast your fun day and those to come at the verrrrrrry fancy **Headlands Coastal Lodge & Spa** (with ocean views and claw-foot tubs if you can splurge on the $$$ for a room) with glasses of crisp white wine and watch the sun turn orange and sink into the ocean from your window bar seat.

HOT TIP: In the 1800s, a hot sailor and his lady love got hitched on the picturesque Proposal Rock in blink-and-you-miss-it Neskowin. Now it can claim two centuries of question-popping moments.

TREASURE SEEKERS

Tackle a shared goal together with an agate hunting trip. Not entirely sure what one looks like IRL? Pop into **Time Capsule Antiques & More** to comb through ancient magazines, play the equally ancient pinball, and stick a pin into the ceiling maps to show where you're from. Everyone gets an agate when they leave, which is handy because you have an identifier as you head off to the hunt. (Pro tip: Shine your phone's flashlight in them to make wild patterns.) Now, of course, there is the obviously named **Agate Beach** with powdery fine sand and a rep for fancy rocks. But some folks say the changing of the shoreline over the years means **Fogarty**

AGATES OF THE OREGON COAST

Creek State Recreation Area is now the go-to spot. Plus, you get to go through a cool tunnel to get to the beach. Celebrate your success or drown the misery with dirt-cheap Bloody Marys and expensive views at the **Clarion Inn Surfrider Resort**'s simple bar.

SEA OF LOVE

Spend an afternoon cruising down the 101 with *Pet Sounds* on the speakers and an ever-changing coastline in the rearview. In Newport, say yowza to the sexy curves of the Yaquina Bay Bridge and head to the **Historic Bayfront** to see dozens of big roly-poly sea lions wrestle on the floating docks like teens trying to get the prime real estate on the couch. Interested in spending the night? The historic **Sylvia Beach Hotel** on Nye Beach is an adorable old-school spot. Each room in the hundred-year-old hotel is themed after a different writer like Agatha Christie or Oscar Wilde. And, no, you won't find any wi-fi or TVs. These rooms are for reading, snogging, or sleeping, and that's it. Just the way Oscar would've wanted it.

Skip into each of the little hamlets as you head south—Seal Rock, Waldport, and Yachats, oh my—ducking into whatever place grabs your attention. Might we suggest combing through the mounds of ship steering wheels, yard fountains, and just . . . stuff at the **Pirate Picker**, or dining at the quaint **Drift Inn** restaurant, which has live music every night of the week.

Finally, keep that lighthouse love going with a visit to another of our state's eleven incandescent beauties. **Heceta Head** is allegedly one of the most photographed lighthouses in the world. And sitting at two hundred feet above the ocean with its Fresnel lens still beaming twenty-one miles out into the sea, we can see why. The hillside hike past the innkeeper quarters with its little garden turns to a cliffside path where you can imagine the keeper hugging the hand railing with a lantern as the fog rolls in, vigilant in keeping the bright light shining so ships can make it safely back to port.

Long Beach

Ironically, a twenty-six-mile-long peninsula in Washington State is the favorite beach of many Oregonians. The place where Lewis and Clark first spotted the Pacific Ocean is still full of wonders, not the least of which is a tiny alligator-man monster that virtually put this region on the map. Wind up your Skee-Ball/oyster-shucking arm and prepare to have some real fun.

SHORE THING

The name **Cape Disappointment** belies the beauty of this windswept point where the Columbia River and the Pacific Ocean crash precariously into each other. This state park has it all: Climb the lighthouse for light-to-medium sea captain role-play, hike through the old-growth forest down to Dead Man's Cove, or briefly make out behind a yurt if you fancy. It also has one of the best semisecret beaches around. Pay the parking fee (no grumbling, it's helping preserve this special spot) before taking a short walk to **Waikiki Beach**. While not quite as tropical as its Hawaiian counterpart, the Pacific Northwest's Waikiki is unequivocally rad in its own way. This small cove is supposedly the actual spot William Clark—you know, the "Lewis and Clark"

Clark—reached the Pacific Ocean in 1805. Its shape keeps it sheltered from winds, and sand traffic is low. Even in March, it's often warm enough to throw down a blanket, roll up your jeans, and bask in the sun. For Pacific Northwest folks, that's a big deal.

Twenty-eight miles of sandy beaches north of the cape deliver both A+ napping and kite-flying opportunities. To cram in all the fun, you'll want to stay at least a night, if not more. The adorbs award goes to **Sou'wester Historic Lodge and Vintage Travel Trailer Resort**. This special spot is a layered onion of lore that begins with a powerful Portland senator, Henry Corbett, who built a vacation lodge in the last breaths of the 1800s. Later it went public, adding itty-bitty cabins and, in 2012, full-on kitsch when Thandi Rosenbaum bought it and turned it into the hideaway wonderland it is today. Now guests can choose between cabins or lodge rooms bedecked with thrifted seascape paintings, or battered and beloved Airstreams like the 1953 "Potato Bug" with its old-timey floral wallpaper, cozy afghans, and dented teakettle. Invite a bunch of friends and stretch out in the sixty-five-year-old "African Queen," perfect for a night of rowdy games. Whatever accommodations you choose (go for the trailers, just sayin'), that's only the beginning of the fun.

Upon check-in, request one of the free record players and grab some vinyl from the giant library in the lodge's communal living room, also the spot for chill puzzle parties, killer live music from some Northwest bests like Ural Thomas and Laura Gibson, and inspiring readings from esteemed authors. After you've stocked your sleeping quarters with music and a bottle of something from the lobby's honor-system shop, you're free to explore Sou'wester's garden sauna, makeshift sound bath, or various trailers turned art galleries, tea nooks, and even a secondhand clothing store. If you have time, borrow bikes and cruise the esplanade through the dunes and into town. You'll want to be back by nightfall when the grounds become a full mix of summer camp and Halloween with people out bopping between trailers by flashlight, sharing drinks by the fire, and making friends. Retire to your tuna can, full and happy to cuddle up to the soothing sounds of crashing waves or raindrops on an aluminum roof.

The quarters are as tight as a submarine, and at some point you'll probably want to venture out. For tooling around town the next day, the main drag has all the beach-town things you want—sweet-smelling waffle cones from the ice-cream shop, a noisy arcade of games, and the "World's Largest Frying Pan,"

which, at fourteen feet high, is no longer the largest but a ridiculous photo op nonetheless. Even if tourist traps aren't your thing, you'd be remiss not to visit **Marsh's Free Museum**.

Turn out your pockets, scour the car's console, and be prepared with quarters, nickels, and dimes to get the full experience. For nine decades, this family-owned Main Street mainstay has entertained visitors with its gift shop/menagerie, which includes creepy taxidermy oddities like an eight-legged lamb, authentic shrunken head, and most famously, Jake the Alligator Man. After you're thoroughly heebie-jeebied, take that coinage and descend upon the collection of antique contraptions and automated peep shows. Drop in dimes to have your fortune told, sneak a peek of "the Sultan's harem," or get the 411 by making your date grip the handle on the love tester machine.

AWWW, SHUCKS

For a dreamy afternoon, the tiny unincorporated time capsule of **Oysterville** is worth an hour or two of your time. Nestled up against the oyster-filled Willapa Bay, this charming neighborhood consists of a number of historic homes built before 1880, which, for the Pacific Northwest, is hella old. Park at the schoolhouse and pay a visit to the steepled church. It's almost always open and almost always hauntingly empty. Take a moment to count your blessings and play a few notes on the public piano. May heaven strike you down with a lightning bolt if you even think of playing "Chopsticks."

Grab a walking map on your way out and take a romantic stroll past the preserved homes and learn their tales. Pause at Mrs. Nelson's sweet garden where crisp, crushed oyster shells form paths around the flower beds, but feel free to skip the downer vibe of Ned Osbourne's house. He was building it for his bride-to-be who jilted him right before the wedding. When she married another man, he stopped construction, never finishing the upstairs and living in sad bachelor decay for the rest of his life. We don't even know how to unpack that one. . . . Instead, let's move along to **Oysterville Sea Farms**, a defunct cannery where hungry tourists can now snap up the day's haul or sip a refreshing rosé on the back patio overlooking the bay. Pour one out for ol' Ned while you're there.

For dinner, **Pickled Fish** is where it's at. Impress your paramour by discreetly checking your phone to find out what time the sun sets and show up twenty minutes prior. The wall of ocean-facing windows and unobstructed vantage point atop the **Adrift Hotel** means you'll have a craft cocktail in hand and the best seat in the house for nature's nightly show. Far from the typical surf-and-turf, the locally focused menu offers a wide range of selections from vegan to Paleo to mounds of french fries. Take your time eating and you might get to enjoy some live music with your dessert. Expect anything from a delightful folk duo to a strutting Journey cover band. Don't stop believin', y'all.

RIDE INTO THE SUNSET

Another day, another chance for sun-filled adventures. (Translation: These activities are best when the weather is on your side.) And on the world's longest contiguous beach, options abound. Pop up the main drag and into the **Funland arcade** for a few rounds of silly fun. Legend says the winner of one thousand Skee-Ball tickets will be the one to rule us all. Once the flashing bells and lights get a little overwhelming, we know *just* the way to mix things up: go and see a man about a horse. One that you can ride.

Next to the Adrift Hotel, **Long Beach Horse Rides** has a sweet little corral and cabin where you can sign up for an afternoon beach ride. They'll help everyone—from total novice to full-fledged equestrian—saddle up a stallion and head out for a two-hour ride. Amble through a coastal forest and tall beach grass before trotting down to the mirrored spot where land, ocean, and sky all come together. It's one for the books.

Post-ride, when you're feeling like a Young Gun, refuel. Take a four-mile drive south to **Ole Bob's** on the harbor in neighboring Ilwaco. The combo seafood market and restaurant hauls in fresh catches every day for hungry visitors to take home or eat in. The area is swimming in goodies—it boasts the largest salmon run in the world and half of Washington's oyster harvest. Plus the requisite halibut, tuna, anchovies, and crabs.

Nab a spot on the patio that overlooks the marina and scarf down some grub while you each pick out your favorite boat with names like *Seaduction*, *Better When Wet*, and *Plunder My Treasure*. If given the opportunity, definitely reenact the "I'm flying!" scene from *Titanic*. That's hot.

Acknowledgments

Thank you to our Joshua Tree family for being part of our biggest love adventure; to our parents for instilling curiosity and ambition; giant hugs to B. Frayn Masters, Zach Dundas, and Sadie Adams for doing the first reads on proposal chapters; to Brian Barker for early support; to Emma Mcilroy and Amy Taylor for night paddling; to Fawn McGee for joining in on an uncomfortable, spider-infested room at a spot that did not make the cut; to the PoMo edit team (especially FEM) for listening to Eden talk about this project too much; to Mark Ray, Rebecca Armstrong, and the whole North family for ceaseless support and untiring light; to Tuck Woodstock and Sylveon Consulting for helping us make sure our words were inclusive; to Conner Reed for giving his approval stamp; to our wonderful and essential couples therapist, Heather Rensmith; and to Corrina Repp for bringing Ashod to the Crystal Ballroom greenroom before a Menomena show, where he met Eden.

More gratitude to the Sasquatch Books crew for letting us fulfill this funny idea we had in the car one day. Thank you to Gary Luke for initial enthusiasm; Jen Worick for being our favorite cat friend, GIF sender, and a truly delightful editor; Jill Saginario for shepherding us through our timeline as the world burned; Tony Ong for turning a zillion illustrations into a beautiful, legible layout; Michelle Hope for her eagle copyediting eye; Alison Keefe for helping this become a real, physical thing; and Nikki Sprinkle and Jenny Abrami for helping people know it actually exists in the world. You are all magic.

We couldn't have gone on all these adventures without the local publications that tirelessly write about our beautiful state. To *Portland Monthly*, Travel Portland, Travel Oregon, *Willamette Week*, *Portland Mercury*, and the *Oregonian*, thank you for all you do. To everyone else, support regional journalism. You won't know what you got until it's gone.

Cheat Sheet

A HANDY GUIDE FOR
FINDING THE
BEST DATE FOR YOU

Index

About the Authors

EDEN DAWN is the style editor for *Portland Monthly*, Oregon's number-one-selling magazine. She is a well-known personality in the community, often seen judging drag queen pageants, sitting on several advisory boards, chatting through live television segments, emceeing fundraising galas, performing at storytelling events, and even hosting her own quarterly series Fashion in Film at the historic Hollywood Theatre.

ASHOD SIMONIAN is a creative director at North, a Portland-based brand strategy and creative agency; co-owner of Imaginary Authors, a niche perfume house; and author of *Real Fun*, a book of photography and stories documenting his decade spent touring the world in various indie rock bands.

Together Eden and Ashod run the activism-based nail polish company Claws Out, which has included collaborations with the Portland Trail Blazers and Elizabeth Warren's presidential campaign. *The Portland Book of Dates* is a natural extension of their adventurous, overextended lifestyle, bringing together Eden's passion for words and Ashod's handcrafted illustrations. They've been married since 2017 and wrote this book from their slightly creaky hundred-year-old house in Portland's Alberta Arts District with their two bossy cats, Ruby and Covered Wagon.

For updates and more fun places to explore, follow us @portlandbookofdates. If you end up making out at any of these places, tag us.